The Adversary Press

ISBN 0-935742-06-9

Printed in the United States of America

Cover and book design by Billie M. Keirstead
Art production by Joe Tonelli

Copies of this publication may be ordered at $3.00 each to cover
printing and mailing from Modern Media Institute, 556 Central
Avenue, St. Petersburg, FL 33701

odern Media Institute
556 Central Avenue
St. Petersburg, Florida 33701

A Modern Media Institute
Ethics Center Seminar

Preface

Nineteen distinguished editors, publishers and scholars gathered in St. Petersburg in December 1982 to test the thesis of one participant: that the press is too hostile in its relationship with government.

Stepping down as president of the American Society of Newspaper Editors, and almost simultaneously as editor of the *New York Daily News,* Michael J. O'Neill told the Society in a May 1982 valedictory address that newspapers had gone too far as adversaries of government and that they should make peace.

The reaction to O'Neill's speech was mixed. Some editors argued that, far from overplaying the role of adversary, the press was if anything too soft. An equal number felt that O'Neill had said something important, something that needed careful consideration.

The Modern Media Institute judged that O'Neill had opened up a subject so important that it should be considered by a small gathering of the best academic and journalistic minds. And so, on the evening of December 3, this group of men and women gathered in a hotel with a splendid view of the Gulf of Mexico for two full days of conversation.

There was no intention of reaching hard and fast conclusions and none was reached. But there was general agreement that the conference had served a worthwhile purpose, and it is hoped that this book will let you share some of the conversation that filled long days on Friday and Saturday, December 4 and 5.

The book includes an overview report of the conference by Charles Stafford, *St. Petersburg Times* national correspondent in Washington, an edited transcript of the proceedings and the O'Neill address which was responsible for it all.

The Modern Media Institute, which sponsored the conference, was founded in 1975 by the late Nelson Poynter, chairman of the *St. Petersburg Times* in Florida and *Congressional Quarterly* in Washington. On his death in 1978, Mr. Poynter bequeathed

stock of the *Times* to MMI which uses its dividends
to support a wide variety of educational programs and
seminars such as this. As the Institute has grown and
matured its principal functions have been grouped into four interrelated centers—Writing, Management,
Graphics and Ethics. A seminar on America's adversary press was a natural assignment for the Ethics
Center as its role and responsibilities continue to
evolve.

Donald K. Baldwin
Modern Media Institute

Participants in the seminar were:

Professor Louis Hodges, Director, Studies in Applied Ethics, Washington and Lee University. He also served as moderator.

Michael J. O'Neill, former editor, *New York Daily News*.

Hodding Carter, former State Department spokesman, presently producer, "The Inside Story" for Public Broadcasting Service.

Harold Evans, former editor of the *Times* and *Sunday Times* of London. Visiting professor at MMI.

James K. Batten, president, Knight-Ridder Newspapers.

William Thomas, editor and executive vice president, *Los Angeles Times*.

James Hoge, publisher, *Chicago Sun-Times*.

Michael Gartner, president, *Des Moines Register*.

Mrs. Katherine Fanning, publisher, *Anchorage Daily News*.

C.K. McClatchy, editor, *Sacramento Bee*.

Martin Linsky, assistant director, Institute of Politics, Kennedy School of Government, Harvard University.

Arthur Caplan, associate for the humanities, The Hastings Center.

Professor Gaye Tuchman, graduate center, Department of Sociology, City College of New York.

Ms. B.J. Phillips, Atlanta correspondent, Time, Inc.

Eugene C. Patterson, editor and president, the *St. Petersburg Times*.

Donald K. Baldwin, director, Modern Media Institute.

Roy Peter Clark, associate director, Modern Media Institute.

Robert Haiman, executive editor, *St. Petersburg Times*.

Marion K. Poynter, member of MMI board of directors.

Contents

Introduction

For two days in early December, a handful of press royalty gathered at a Florida round table to examine the O'Neill proposition.

It was more debate than inquisition, though there was a touch of that about it. Michael J. O'Neill, lately editor of the *New York Daily News,* was given a seat and asked to explain himself.

He said some had misunderstood him. But he backed down not a whit from the premise he posited in his valedictory to the American Society of Newspaper Editors last May, to wit: "The press has become so adversarial in its relationship with government that it threatens the democratic process."

Seventeen others—editors, publishers, reporters and academics—were present at the Modern Media Institute seminar in St. Petersburg Beach. The debate was lively, the consensus lean.

O'Neill's Lincoln had his Douglas—Michael Gartner, president of the *Des Moines Register.* The remainder of the group took positions between their two poles, finding grist in the O'Neill argument, but chaff also.

The few areas of agreement were these:

1) The press has a poor public image, and must improve it or risk regulation. The degree of risk remained in contention.

2) An important cause of the public's animosity is the needlessly adversarial, ill-mannered behavior of some reporters, particularly those caught by the eye of the television camera.

3) Ethical behavior and acceptable reportorial technique should not be prescribed by codes of conduct or other written documents, but by example.

4) In too many cases, editors have surrendered their news judgment function to reporters.

Included in the gathering, which was made welcome by Eugene C. Patterson, editor and president of the *St. Petersburg Times* and board chairman of

Modern Media Institute, were: Hodding Carter III,
producer of public television's "The Inside Story,"
former newspaper editor, and State Department
spokesman in the Carter administration; Harold
Evans, former editor of the *Times* of London and the
Sunday Times; William Thomas, editor of the *Los
Angeles Times;* James K. Batten, president of Knight-
Ridder Newspapers; James Hoge, publisher of the
Chicago Sun-Times; Katherine Fanning, publisher of
the *Anchorage Daily News;* C.K. McClatchy, editor
of the *Sacramento Bee;* Martin Linsky, assistant direc-
tor of Harvard's Institute of Politics; Arthur Caplan,
associate for the humanities at the Hastings Center;
Gaye Tuchman, City College of New York sociologist;
Time Correspondent B.J. Phillips; *St. Petersburg
Times* Executive Editor Robert Haiman; Marion K.
Poynter, widow of Modern Media Institute's founder,
Nelson Poynter, and a member of the MMI board of
directors; MMI Director Donald K. Baldwin and
Associate Director Roy Peter Clark.

Louis Hodges, director of Studies in Applied Ethics
at Washington and Lee University, was the
moderator.

Benjamin C. Bradlee, executive editor of the
Washington Post, was a ghostly presence. His letter
to Patterson, regretting his inability to attend,
established the environment of the seminar.

"Someone has got to answer Mike," said Bradlee.
"I thought his argument was really flawed...trendy,
establishmentarian, and just plain wrong....

"Mike talks about the press's harshly adversarial
posture towards government. Baloney. I'd like to talk
about the selling of the presidency, the manipulation
of the public, where the press is a captive, if not willing, victim. I agree with what Scotty Reston said five
or ten years ago...that far from being too aggressive,
the press is not being aggressive enough. I think the
press, and that includes us, is so goddamn scared now
of its new image as all-powerful, that we are being
too timid. I suggest that the press has been easier on
Reagan than on any president in my memory...."

Perhaps there is a small danger in "post-Watergate" journalism in which every reporter wants to become a Woodward or Bernstein, Bradlee said, but editors exist to eliminate that danger.

"Does anyone really want to make peace with government?" Bradlee asked. "Do you really want us to formalize a 'more positive, more tolerant' attitude with government? More tolerant of what? More tolerant of lying? More tolerant of misrepresentation? More tolerant of manipulation, photo opportunities? That can't be serious. That's a pact with the devil."

Having read that, O'Neill said, "I feel like handing in my sword."

His starting point was not the performance of the press, but the poor performance of the American system, he said. Capacity to govern has been crippled by "the intensely adversarial culture that we have in this country; not just the press, the whole culture."

But the press, because of its power and its championship of the adversarial culture, has done more than most groups to set the quarrelsome tone, he said.

"Inasmuch as journalists are part of the problem," O'Neill said, "we should make some effort to solve it. We can't just keep passing ourselves off as eunuchs in the throne room. We have to, and I think we can, commit some acts of citizenship without violating any royal decrees of our profession.

"Now this makes me an establishmentarian, to use Ben Bradlee's $6 word (that's an awfully big word for Ben). Well, so be it."

Gartner told O'Neill his speech was brave and eloquent, but wrong.

The press, he said, should not make peace with government or any other segment of society. It should be concerned with the truth and accuracy of what it writes and the weight it gives to each story, but not with the consequences. Consensus and conciliation are desirable goals, Gartner said, but the path to them goes through the adversarial process.

There was a great deal of thrashing about in search of a definition of "adversarial process" acceptable to all, but none was found. Some said it need not be nasty, others that it was inherently nasty. Some said truth was its goal, others compromise.

Prof. Linsky, looking to consequences, said the state of press freedom for the next half-century could be decided by the debate ignited by O'Neill. Abuse of press power will lead to loss of credibility and inevitably to curbs on that power, he said. Society gave the First Amendment, and society can take it away.

Hoge thought Linsky was overstating the danger. Sure people hate the press, he said, but they understand its utility. Recent adverse libel decisions are symptomatic of the public's skepticism of the power of the press, he said, but there is a vast difference in this kind of incremental tightening of the environment in which the press performs and repeal of the First Amendment.

Carter returned to square one, labeling the notion of an all-powerful press a myth. He said he couldn't think of a single issue the press had anticipated and set on the public agenda, or a single instance, including Watergate, in which it had a major impact on society.

Rather than fearing the power of the press, Carter said, public officials have a continuing sense that the press regularly fails the test of fairness and accuracy.

He disputed a Hoge statement that the press has been moving in recent years to diagnose and correct problems through self-examination. It stopped creating news councils and hiring ombudsmen when it stopped worrying about Richard Nixon and Spiro Agnew, he said.

But it should be attending its problems, Carter said, because it is a monopolistic public utility in a society that has regulated every other monopolistic public utility.

At the very least, he said, newspapers should be looking over each other's shoulders and criticizing coverage. There is a public perception that the press is a club that closes ranks rather than concede error among its own members, he said.

Hoge and Carter crossed swords again over the impact of television on the press function.

Carter said TV, which is national in a way no newspaper is national and superficial in a way that helps government, has been used by government to bypass the print medium. By intelligent use of TV, he said, government can seize the high ground in policy discussion, reaching over the heads of the press to the public, turning discussion on and off like a tap.

Hoge said this might be the case, but the impact is far less than government should expect. While people might think TV is their main source of news, he said, closer examination shows that it remains newspapers.

He criticized TV news for its fixation with mayhem, its obsession with confrontational game playing with government officials, and with its short story construction that requires a beginning and an end, good guys and bad guys.

TV news creates distance between the people and government by giving viewers a feeling that government is theater in which they are not involved. This leads, Hoge said, to alienation.

There was general agreement that television news focuses more on events than issues.

On the morning of the second day, the group returned to MMI's roundtable—marvelous dedication since just beyond the windows a benevolent sun warmed the white sand beach to summer-like comfort—to discuss the proposition that the sailors have seized the ship.

Batten said some reporters feel driven to expose graft even where none exists, and that editors often defer rather than block such "noble effort." It might well be, he said, that editors have permitted democracy in the newsroom to get out of hand. They confuse high morale with leadership, he said.

An editor needs to listen to his reporters' suggestions, for they are the eyes and the ears of the newspaper, but he must make the decisions, Batten said.

Clark, whose duties as a writing coach and researcher have taken him into newsrooms throughout the country, said there are three kinds of newspapers.

He labeled them the *Nina,* the *Pinta,* and the *Santa Maria.*

Aboard the *Nina,* he said, reporters make decisions because the editors have abdicated their responsibilities. Stories go into the paper without editing.

The *Pinta,* Clark said, is a newspaper of the editor, by the editor, and for the editor. Reporters never have ideas, only assignments that come from the editors' meetings. Reporters fail when they do not deliver a story that meets an editor's preconceived idea of what it should be.

The *Santa Maria* is that newsroom where editors and reporters work as a harmonious team, where the code words for responsibility—collaboration, flexibility, communication, and the inheritance of values—have meaning. This is the best kind of ship to sail on, Clark said, but it is rare.

Leadership is the key, said Haiman. Reporters, he said, regard themselves as the keepers of the flame—the defenders of the newspaper's honor and honesty. When a good, tough-minded editor comes aboard, the reporters turn down the flame and follow him but if he is succeeded by a less talented editor, the flame will be turned up again, Haiman said.

The group came back again to a subject that nagged at them throughout the two days of discussion — the behavior of reporters in seeking the news, and its effects on the public's image of the press. Too often, they agreed, behavior is misbehavior, questioning is needlessly confrontational, privacy is invaded, personal rights are trampled, victims are treated without compassion.

O'Neill said he thought the biggest offenders were television reporters. But Ms. Phillips said newspaper reporters have begun covering stories the way TV covers them, and that leads to adversarial journalism.

Because television, the originator of "ambush journalism," has only 45 seconds to report a story, the most efficacious way to do it is to establish a confrontation, she said. Ethical values are shaped by the necessity of getting it live on camera.

Mike Wallace, with his abrasive interviewing technique, is the role model for young reporters throughout the country, she said.

How can reporters be taught better manners, better techniques?

The news executives agreed that the teaching should not be attempted with codes of ethics or conduct or other written commandments.

Example is the best teacher, said Patterson. When a reporter receives advice from an editor, when an editor is reprimanded for permitting a reporter's bad judgment to get into print, the word spreads through the newsroom and, in time, a set of values is formed.

An atmosphere of compassion and concern for accuracy cannot be described on paper, said Mrs. Fanning, but can only be communicated by example.

True, said O'Neill. It is important to create a total atmosphere. But communication among officers and sailors is a prime requirement and there is often too little of it as the newsroom moves from news crisis to news crisis.

Near the end of it all, Evans counseled his American cousins to keep up the good fight to improve performance, to improve the public's appreciation of a free press, to resist regulation.

In Britain and other European countries, he said, inertia, habit, and lousy behavior have led to restriction of the press through a succession of common law decisions and statutes.

It is important that the American press win, Evans said, "because you are still the only laboratory in the world for what a free press can do."

Charles Stafford
National Correspondent
St. Petersburg Times

Power of the Press

A Problem for the Republic–a Challenge for Editors

Michael J. O'Neill

American Society of Newspaper Editors

May 5, 1982

Standing on the gallows for the last five months, waiting for the trap door to fall, has been a stimulating experience. As Samuel Johnson once remarked, the prospect of being hanged does powerfully concentrate the mind. In my case, I couldn't help thinking about the mortality of newspapers—the *Daily News,* of course—but also other troubled newspapers and, indeed, newspapers in general because they are probably all quite mortal.

There are in most of us those intimations of immortality that Wordsworth wrote about. We never think of ourselves as ending, just as little children cannot conceive of their parents dying. And so it is with institutions, from large corporations to great cities. We assume they will last forever.

Except if you walk through the ruins of Ephesus in Asia Minor, and realize that a population of 250,000 simply vanished into history, you are reminded of the fragile nature of man and his works. And you get the same feeling, in a more intimate way, when newspapers suddenly disappear. Particularly the ones you have known and loved.

Under these circumstances, it is natural to reflect on our business—to consider what forces are working for its improvement or disparagement, how we are faring generally in the social and economic turmoil now buffeting us all. An editor is inspired to reflect especially on the state of his profession and, in my case, to worry about how well we are fulfilling our obligations to the society we serve. For while there has been an astonishing growth in the power of the media over the last decade or so, I am by no means sure we are using it wisely. The tendency has been to revel in the power and wield it freely rather than to accept any corresponding increase in responsibility.

In fact, the very processes we use to inform the public have been badly distorted by television and, to a lesser degree, by a whole range of other phenomena from investigative excesses to our enthrallment with adversary journalism. So not only have we failed to match new responsibility to new power, we have also yielded to trends that are hurting the cause of a well informed citizenry.

The extraordinary powers of the media, most convincingly displayed by network television and the national press, have been mobilized to influence major public issues and national elections, to help diffuse the authority of Congress and to disassemble the political parties—even to make presidents or to break them. Indeed, the media now weigh so heavily on the scales of power that some political scientists claim we are upsetting the historic checks and balances invented by our forefathers.

Samuel P. Huntington of Harvard has observed that "during the '60s and '70s, the media were the institution whose power expanded most significantly and that posed the most serious challenges to governmental authority." Max M. Kampelman has similarly warned that "the relatively unrestrained power of the media may well represent an even greater challenge to democracy than the much publicized abuses of power by the executive and the Congress." And Sen. Daniel P. Moynihan, who concedes the press already has the upper hand in Washington, says that if the balance should tip too far in its direction "our capacity for effective democratic government will be seriously and dangerously weakened."

This is flattering, of course, because all newspapermen dream of being movers and shakers and the thought that we may actually be threatening the national government is inspirational. In several respects, it is also true. The Communications Revolution, which is profoundly reshaping all of Western society, has also altered the basic terms of reference between the press and American democracy.

No longer are we just the messengers, observers on the sidelines, witch's mirrors faithfully telling society how it looks. Now we are deeply imbedded in the democratic process itself, as principal actors rather than bit players or mere audience.

No longer do we merely cover the news. Thanks mainly to television, we are often partners now in the creation of news—unwilling and unwitting partners, perhaps, but partners nonetheless in producing what Daniel Boorstin has deplored as pseudo events, pseudo protests, pseudo crises and controversies.

No longer do we look on government only with the healthy skepticism required by professional tradition. Now we have a hard, intensely adversarial attitude. We treat the government as the enemy—and government officials as convenient targets for attack and destroy missions.

No longer do we submit automatically to the rigors of old-fashioned impartiality. Now, not always but too often, we surrender to the impulse of advocacy, in the name of reform but forgetful of balance, fairness and—if it isn't too unfashionable to say so—what is good for the country.

These trends, however, are more symptom that cause. Much deeper processes are at work. The mass media, especially television, are not only changing the way government is covered but the way it functions. The crucial relationship between the people and their elected representatives—the very core of our political system—has been altered fundamentally.

In ways that Jefferson and Hamilton never intended nor could even imagine, Americans now have the whole world delivered to them every day, in pulsating, living color—all of life swept inside their personal horizon. Distant events—Selma, Alabama...the riot-torn Democratic convention in Chicago...the hostages in Iran—are instant experiences, neither insulated by a reporter's translation nor muted by what Theodore H. White has called the consoling "filter of time."

The flashing images mobilize popular emotions on a truly massive scale and with stunning speed, quickly generating and shaping public opinion. The televised battle scenes from Vietnam, as we know, aroused a whole nation against the war, helped reverse our national policy, and ultimately destroyed the presidency of Lyndon Johnson.

"The introduction of modern mass communications," said the sociologist Daniel Bell, "allows us, in many cases forces us, to respond directly and immediately to social issues."

Television has thus played a decisive role in the so-called revolution of rising expectations. It has strongly stimulated the consumption culture. It has dramatized the gap between haves and have nots, helping to create a runaway demand for more and more government services and for equality of result as well as of opportunity.

Time and time again, presidents discover that the public has already made up its mind about issues before they have even had time to consider them. Their hand is forced. The deliberative process that representative government was designed to assure is frustrated.

Television has also indelibly changed the democratic process by establishing a direct communication link between political leaders and their constituents. Now, as never before, these politicians are able to bypass the print media and the troublesome business of depending on reporters to represent them to the public.

More significant, but for the same reason, they are also able to bypass their parties so that the whole system of party government, built up over nearly two centuries, is now breaking down. This, in turn, is contributing to the crisis of government that Lloyd Cutler and others find so threatening to the American system.

In presidential elections, that most central of democratic functions, media appeal has replaced party screening in the primary selection process. National conventions are no longer relevant. Most of the subtle bonds of political power, whether the ritual dispensing of favors or dependence on party for advancement, have been snapped. From the district clubhouse to Washington, especially Washington, political discipline has almost disappeared.

The president no longer has much leverage over the members of Congress, even those in his own party. Congress itself is in a disheveled state with power so diluted that neither floor leaders nor committee chairmen are able to act with the authority, for example, of a Sam Rayburn.

As a consequence, power has been badly fractured. Our capacity for achieving consensus on national issues has been damaged. George F. Kennan cites fragmented authority as one of the chief causes of the disarray in U.S. foreign policy, and he mainly blames Washington's over-reaction to popular emotions whipped up by the media.

Where power is frayed, as Douglass Cater has pointed out, "public opinion is called on more regularly than elsewhere to act as arbiter among competing policies and politicians." So we have the paradox of the mass media tearing down power on the one hand, and then gaining power themselves at the expense of the institutions they have diminished.

One of the victims of this process is the presidency itself. Although many complex forces have conspired to undermine its authority, television and the national press have played a major role. For one thing, they have focused tremendous attention on the president, as the personal symbol of the nation and its ideals, as the principal instrument of action and the first resort of complaint or redress. They also rely on him for the drama, the glamor and excitement, that television forever craves and must have to survive. Indeed, he happily conspires in the creation of media events and makes all sorts of other concessions in order to present his deeds in a way that TV finds congenial.

A skilled communicator like Ronald Reagan is a master of television. He exploits it with great effect to project himself and his policies directly to millions of people, going over the heads of Congress and, incidentally, making an end run around newspapers.

But television can also be cruel. It raises public expectations far beyond the president's reach and then, when he cannot satisfy them, it magnifies the perception of failure. By massive over-exposure, the media also strip away the protective mystery of the Oval Office, inviting the same kind of premature disenchantment that destroys so many TV stars.

A more serious concern is how the media merry-go-round is distorting the news, the information base, if you will, that people need to make sound decisions in a democracy. The capacity to mobilize public opinion is now so great that issues and events are often shaped as much to serve the media's demands as to promote the general welfare.

The result is a blurring of the line between the medium and the message. Between substance and shadow, like the shadow on Plato's cave. "In the beginning," as Huntington has commented, "television covered the news; soon, news was produced for television." Boorstin has made the same point, but less politely.

Unfortunately, television is an impressionistic medium that marshals images and emotions rather than words and reasons. Its lenses are distorting. They focus on the dramatic and the visible, on action and conflict. News decisions are influenced by what film is available, what events "project" well, what can be explained easily in quickie bursts of audio headlines.

Newsmakers modify their behavior to fit, creating controversy on demand, turning away from debate and petition in favor of protest and demonstration. As the former Tammany Hall chief, Edward N. Costikyan, put it in a manual for political candidates: "Television reporting is not news, it is spectacle. To capture coverage, you must create a spectacle...." Some issues, artificial or real, are churned up to the point that they command national attention and affect national policy. Other issues which may be far more valid and important—lagging investment in basic research, for example—are ignored because they cannot be seen by television's beady red eye.

The raw materials of public deliberation thus become a confusing mixture of the real and unreal, important and irrelevant—a jumble of impressions that confound even the historians. Arthur M. Schlesinger Jr. said that after being involved in the making of history during his White House days, he could never again rely on the testimony of the press.

So we all spin around in a vicious circle. Television first changes the nature of mass communication, including communication between the people and their government. In response, political leaders, single issue groups, and all other players on the public stage change their media behavior. Then the media, including the national press, react and interact. Masses of people become involved, contributing to the surge of participatory democracy that students of government have decried. Public agendas and priorities are distorted. The thrust of the news, the pace, and even the content of the news, become captive to the process.

Adding to the general turmoil are two other phenomena: the press's harshly adversarial posture toward government and its infatuation with investigative reporting. These attitudes, which have always lurked in the psyche of American journalists, were enormously intensified by Vietnam, Watergate and the general attack on authority in the 1960s and 1970s. Both news coverage and the conduct of government have been duly affected—but not improved.

It may be foolhardy to say anything uncharitable about investigative reporting; it is in such vogue now. We have all basked in the glory of exposés and gloated while public officials have turned slowly on the spit of newspaper disclosures. I remember the triumph we felt at the *Daily News* when we reported that a congressman had lied about pleading the Fifth Amendment and then saw him destroyed as candidate for mayor.

On balance, investigative reporting has probably done more good than harm, although a wise member of the *New York Times* editorial board, Roger Starr, would dispute the point. He once suggested wistfully that journalism schools should ban Lincoln Steffens' famous book, *The Shame of the Cities.* He said that muckraking did so much damage to the cities that he hated to think what havoc modern investigative reporters might commit.

Muckraking has been over-emphasized, tending to crowd out other more significant kinds of reporting. If we had not been so busy chasing corrupt officials, we might not be guilty of having missed some of the biggest stories of the last half century:

• The great migration of blacks from the South to the industrial cities of the North, something we didn't discover until there were riots in the streets of Detroit.

• The first mincing steps toward war in Vietnam, which we did not begin reporting seriously until our troops were involved.

• The women's liberation movement and the massive migration of women into the job market, a social revolution that we originally dismissed as an outbreak of bra burning.

In some cases, investigative reporting has also run off the ethical tracks. Individuals and institutions have been needlessly hurt when the lure of sensational headlines has prevailed over fairness, balance, and a valid public purpose. Those uninspiring scenes of reporters and cameramen trampling over Richard Allen's front lawn to hound his wife and children raise questions.

Is our duty to inform so stern that we must exile ourselves from our own humanity? Are we like policemen who have become inured to violence? Have we become so cynical, so hardened by our experiences with sham, that we can no longer feel what an official feels, what his wife and children feel, when he is being ripped and torn on TV and in the press? Have we become so arrogant with our power, so competitive, that we cannot decide that the public crime is often not worth the private punishment? That the First Amendment is often abused rather than served by those who would defend it?

"...Is it not true," Kampelman asked, "that no man is free if he can be terrorized by his neighbor? And, is it not possible for words as well as swords to terrorize?"

Similar questions need to be asked about our intensely adversarial coverage of government because this, too, is falsely coloring the information flowing to the public.

We are probably the most adversarial people in the world— "the most anti-American," to quote the British poet Stephen Spender—and we are getting worse all the time. The reasons lie deep in the past—in the Enlightenment's victory over authority, in the romantic concept so eloquently expressed by Milton that truth will triumph in any struggle between reason and falsehood, in the industrial age's emphasis on competition to sort out good products from bad, in the checks and balances built into our own federal system, and in the egalitarian movement that has recently reached such a crescendo in the United States.

In our profession, there are more immediate causes. There are the natural tensions between a president who paints a rosy view of all he does and the messengers who deliver bad news. There is the understandable resentment of officials who feel the media always emphasize the exceptional and negative over the positive, conflict and failure over success. And on the other side, there are the endless official lies and deceits and masquerades that gnaw at the moral intent of reporters.

Within the American context, these tendencies are normal. But they have become more destructive in the last few years. With Vietnam and Watergate, with new waves of young, committed reporters moving into the profession, with older editors feeling guilty about having been "too soft" in the past, the media's relations with government have taken a sharp turn for the worse. The government has become the enemy.

A regretful Vermont Royster has said that the great difference between the Washington press corps of his day and the one now is that then "we did not think of ourselves and the government as enemies."

"We were cynical about much in government, yes," he said. "We were skeptical about many government programs, yes. We thought of ourselves as the watchdogs of government, yes. We delighted in exposés of bungling and corruption, yes. But enemies of government, no."

By the time Jimmy Carter was elected, the critic Anthony Smith has observed, the American press had come "to think of itself as an opposition, almost in the European sense, as a counter-power, part of whose raison d'etre consisted in the constant search for ways to dethrone the incumbent in office."

Smith may have overstated his point, but the adversarial pendulum has in fact swung too far and this is not good for the press, the government, or society. Contrary to 18th century myth and our own litigious tradition, the adversarial method does not necessarily produce truth. As often as not, it misses the truth and distorts reality. And knee-jerk opposition to government by a free press is only a mirror image of the undeviating governmental support that we criticize in the totalitarian media.

In its more extreme forms, the adversarial attitude creates barriers to the clear observation and analysis necessary for objectivity. It encourages emotional involvement with individual personalities and issues. It invites arrogance. It tempts reporters to harrass officials. Ultimately, it undermines credibility because people intuitively sense when the press is being unfair. They are quick to detect a belligerent tone in a story and then discount it in their own mental ledger. And they become deeply skeptical, in Ben J. Wattenberg's view, when all they get from the press is an endless rat-a-tat-tat of failure.

"Is it so absurd to suggest," he asks, "that if all one reads and all one sees is cast under the rubric of crisis and chaos that Americans will either a) believe the press and think America is on the wrong track or b) believe their own senses and think the press and the crisis-mongers they headline are elite, arrogant and so far out of touch as to be non-credible and, even worse, irrelevant?"

If the credibility of news coverage has been hurt, the functioning of government has been damaged even more. Not only are public issues and priorities strongly influenced by the media, every policy initiative, every action, has to run a gauntlet of criticism that is often generated—and always amplified—by the press. In the searing glare of daily coverage, an official's every personal flaw, every act, every mistake, every slip of the tongue, every display of temper, is recorded, magnified, and ground into the public consciousness.

The protests of special interest groups, the charges of publicity-hungry congressmen, are rock-and-rolled through the halls of power. Controversy and conflict are sought out wherever they can be found, sapping energies and usually diverting attention from more urgent public business.

In this whirling centrifuge of criticism and controversy, authority is dissipated. Officials are undermined and demoralized. The capacity to govern, already drastically reduced by the fragmentation of power, is weakened still further.

The media have, in short, made a considerable contribution to the disarray in government and therefore have an obligation to help set matters straight. Or at least to improve them. The corollary of increased power is increased responsibility. The press cannot stand apart, as if it were not an interested party, not to say participant, in the democratic process.

We should begin with an editorial philosophy that is more positive, more tolerant of the frailties of human institutions and their leaders, more sensitive to the rights and feelings of individuals—public officials as well as private citizens.

We should be less arrogant, recognizing our own impressive shortcomings and accepting Walter Lippmann's lament that we can never claim to be the merchants of truth when we so rarely know what the truth is.

We should make peace with the government; we should not be its enemy. No code of chivalry requires us to challenge every official action out of Pavlovian distrust of authority or on the false premise that attack is the best way to flush out truth. Our assignment is to report and explain issues, not decide them. We are supposed to be the observers, not the participants—the neutral party, not the permanent political opposition.

We should cure ourselves of our adversarial mind-set. The adversarial culture is a disease attacking the nation's vital organs. The lawyers will never escape it, but we must. We should retain a healthy skepticism, yes. Provide socially responsible criticism, yes. But relentless hostility? No.

Reporters and editors are much more attracted to failure than to success. An expression of sympathy, perhaps, because failure is always an orphan while success has many fathers. Yet, if we are truly to provide a balanced view of the world, we must tame our negative nature; we need to celebrate success and progress, not just wallow in mankind's woes.

For if we are always downbeat—if we exaggerate and dramatize only the negatives in our society—we attack the optimism that has always been a well-spring of American progress. We undermine public confidence and, without intending it, become a cause rather than just a reporter of national decline.

We should also develop a more sensitive value system to be sure we do not needlessly hurt public figures while exaggerating the public's right to know. Rights do not have to be exercised, just because they exist or because there is a story to be told. The claim of editorial duty should not be a coverup for titillation. Legitimate public need should be weighed against personal harm because, among other things, the fear of media harassment is already seriously affecting recruitment for public service.

Editors also need to be ruthless in ferreting out the subtle biases—cultural, visceral, and ideological—that still slip into copy, into political stories, mostly, but also into the coverage of emotional issues like nuclear power and abortion. Lingering traces of advocacy are less obvious than Janet Cooke's fiction but, for that reason, are more worrisome. Editors—myself included—have simply not exercised enough control over subeditors and reporters reared in the age of the new journalism.

The problem of television is formidable. Its baleful effect on both government and journalism is beyond repeal. The expanding network news shows and the

proliferation of cable promise even more change, con-
fusion, and competition for the attention of busy
Americans. And there are no solutions that I can
think of, only the possibility of limited damage
control.

The key to this is to emphasize the basics, the
things newspapers have always been able to do better than television, services that will become even
more important as the electronic networks continue
swarming over the mass market and, in the process,
define a more specialized role for newspapers.

We should be more resistant than ever to media
hype—the pseudo event, the phoney charges, the stag-
ed protest, the packaged candidate, the prime-time an-
nouncement and televised interviews. Indeed, we
should expose these as vigorously as we expose official
corruption. For it is our job to cut through the superficial to identify the substantive—to explain and
clarify the news, as most newspapers already do, in
a reasoned way that television cannot. Although we
should be interesting, we should not try to be an entertainment like television because this would be both
futile and out of keeping with our special purpose.

Another issue is accountability. A brooding Ray
Price, formerly of the *New York Herald Tribune* and
the White House, complained that the press had ac-
quired power "out of all proportion" to its ability or
inclination to use it responsibly. Walter Wriston, a
banker speaking for many in public life, warned that
the media should remember that "the effective functioning of a democracy requires the most difficult of
all disciplines, self-discipline."

"The freedom of us all," he said, "rides with the
freedom of the press. Nevertheless, its continued
freedom and ours will ultimately depend upon the
media not exploiting to the fullest their unlimited
power."

All sorts of remedies have been proposed, from ombudsmen to news councils, even anti-trust legislation.
Many critics think it would be wonderful if we were
just professionals so there could be the kind of self-
policing that doctors and lawyers have—an uninspir-

ing idea, though, when you consider how few doctors or lawyers are ever disciplined.

The fact is that no grievance committees or councils or laws will really work if the general attitude of the profession is not supportive. If the attitude is right, however, all the clanking machinery is probably unnecessary. Our best defense against opponents, our best bet for strengthening reader credibility, is an openness of mind that encourages both self-examination and outside criticism.

With this psychic base, we can expect editors—miracle of miracles—to respond more constructively to complaints, reporters to be more accepting of direction and correction. We can expect a more aggressive pursuit of fairness and a willingness to provide a more effective right of reply than letters to the editor or an occasional op-ed piece.

In the final analysis, what we need most of all in our profession is a generous spirit, infused with human warmth, as ready to see good as to suspect wrong, to find hope as well as cynicism, to have a clear but uncrabbed view of the world. We need to seek conciliation, not just conflict, consensus, not just disagreement, so that society has a chance to solve its problems. So that we as a nation can find again the common trust and unity—so that we can rekindle the faith in ourselves and in our democracy—that we so urgently need to overcome the great challenges we face in the 1980s.

The Adversary Press

OPENING STATEMENTS BY:

Michael O'Neill
Michael Gartner
Martin Linsky

LOUIS HODGES: We're here, of course, to discuss ethical issues, to engage in ethical discourse. And I've learned through some experience with this kind of thing that it's not always clear just what ethical discourse is. It turns out that when you mix up philosophers and professionals you find out that they use the word "ethics" in different ways. Some people regard ethics as something that you have or don't have. You behave either ethically or unethically.

One way of thinking of ethics is to think in terms of ethical or unethical conduct. Actually, what that means is righteous or unrighteous conduct. Before the fundamentalist preachers messed up our language, we had some perfectly good words and didn't have to use words like ethical and unethical. We could talk about sin and righteousness, but we no longer can do that.

Another way of thinking of ethics is that ethics is not so much something you *have* as it is something you *do*. It's an activity in which you engage. That is, ethics is reasoned discourse about matters of right and wrong, about matters of moral values and moral principles. Reasoned discourse about right and wrong is talk about what people ought to do to each other, about the way we ought to behave toward each other. It's "ought" talk. "Ought," as you know, is an archaic past tense of the verb "to owe." Thus, when we talk in terms of "ought," we're dealing with the question of what it is we owe.

Thus, the topic of our two-day seminar is to raise the question about what the press owes, what we as journalists owe to others in terms of our behavior towards them.

I've discovered that, amazingly, we agree on the values and the moral principles that ought to guide us. Where we disagree is on strategies and methods of implementing them.

We agree, for example, that we ought to keep promises. Yet we disagree about promises made to sources to protect confidentiality and we disagree about whether we need a shield law to implement the keeping of promises or to encourage the keeping of promises.

We know and we agree that we have a duty to the truth. But we disagree about many aspects of the gathering of the truth, the conditions under which it's appropriate or inappropriate, right or wrong to invade someone's privacy in order to get the truth. So our agreements are, I think, much stronger than our disagreements. We're agreed on the basic principles and goals; not agreed on the methods of achieving them and the strategies for going about it.

The first topic is the adversary press and this is a discussion centering on Michael O'Neill's speech.

MICHAEL O'NEILL: Actually, I feel pretty intimidated. As a matter of fact, I feel more like giving out my resume than trying to justify all these crazy things I said last spring. I don't think I'm going to try to argue the points I made earlier. The starting point, actually, was not so much the performance of the press, good or bad, but the poor performance of our country, the American system. I think this is the greatest crisis we now face as a nation. I think it's greater than the recession because, in fact, the recession is *in part* a consequence of this systemic problem.

The fact is, our society is not functioning well. Our capacity to govern, from the remotest congressional district to the Oval Office, is badly crippled. All are trapped in a great political gridlock. Nobody can get anything done; the president, the Congress and the executive departments are all hopelessly entangled in insatiable public demands and desires, conflicting needs, squabbling, single issue groups, fragmented power. In a time of economic failure and nuclear risk, we really cannot now deal with the dangers we confront.

Lloyd Cutler, Cy Vance, and a lot of other people in and out of government, have voiced their alarm about this and are struggling to find solutions. But the outlook, in my view, is not very promising because the causes are built right into the building blocks of democracy. They're locked in the political and cultural contradictions that are both the glory and the misery of our system—contradictions that center mainly on the conflict between our ideals of individual freedom and equality on the one hand, and on the other our need for some kind of central, governing authority.

These conflicts were very troubling to our founding fathers and to such other people as de Tocqueville and Walter Lippmann.

One of the central elements of this dilemma is the intensely adversarial culture we have in this country, not just the press, but the whole culture. And from the spreading plague of lawyers to clashing demands for ever more individual rights and services this is unique in the world. It is an increasing threat to effective government.

Reporters and editors are really champions, of course, in the adversarial culture, despite their self-assumed uniqueness. They are really carried along, like everybody else, by the ebb and flow of social conflict. But they claim it as a professional duty to collide with authority and because of their power, they do more than most other groups, it seems to me, to set the quarrelsome tone of national discourse, not only the tone of the discourse but the direction of policy because the expanded and still growing power of the media heavily impacts on policy formation and decision making and even on the democratic process itself.

Whether you think this is helping or hurting the nation depends on how enthralled you are with the adversarial culture and our unruly role in it. One view is that the press process is a magnificent tool for informing the public and it should be used aggressively without ever trying to guess in advance how it might affect the country or our institutions.

But another position, which I am leaning toward more and more now, is that the adversarial impulses in our society as a whole have been carried to such a destructive extreme that we urgently need to move back toward consensus and conciliation if we are to deal successfully with the great dangers we face in the 1980s.

The corollary of this is that inasmuch as journalists are part of the problem, they should make some effort to solve it. We can't just keep passing ourselves off as eunuchs in the throneroom. We have to, and I think we can, commit some acts of citizenship without violating any great royal decrees of our profession.

Now, this makes me an establishmentarian. But I'm comforted to note that there are others in our business who share at least some of these feelings, including even the alien idea that we have some responsibility to encourage a more conciliatory atmosphere in the country.

It's argued that these concerns have been overtaken by progress and that the journalistic excesses of the immediate post-Watergate period have given way to a calmer, more balanced, less pugnacious kind of journalism.

Journalism has, indeed, moved slowly down the slope from the great peaks of arrogance that followed Watergate. But I think this is less the result of reform than a reflection of a general retreat throughout society from the extraordinary tensions and violent conflicts that marked the 1960s and 1970s. It is a characteristic of American society, and probably other societies, that periods of great social, economic and military activism are followed by periods of slack. Ideas run out of gas, passions are exhausted when problems and frustrations persist and when the spirit is too depleted to deal with them.

In my view, this is our condition now. The small decline we see in the adversarial index is more a measure of this than of basic societal improvement or a fundamental change in journalistic practice.

The Westmoreland case, the militant techniques of programs like *60 Minutes,* the bullying tactics of a Sam Donaldson, the catch-a-thief type of treatment that we gave to Raymond Donovan are evidence, I think, that the temptations of excess still are with us.

Tom Johnson has talked about persistent cases of irresponsible and prejudicial reporting. Jim Batten is worried not so much about great, spectacular failures like Janet Cooke but about more subtle lapses in reporting and editing, inaccuracies, self-righteousness, et cetera.

We recognize that these things are undesirable because we measure them against standards we've already accepted. If we were all to agree now, as a profession, that the adversary process has been carried too far in American society and overvalued by newspapers, we would presumably change our standards to fit. Some practices now considered to be entirely benign would be reclassified as undesirable. As an example, let me cite what Gloria Steinem has called the "prize-fight school of journalism," something which she says produced so much phoney opposition to the ERA that the amendment never had a chance. What she is talking about, of course, is our habit of converting every public issue into a slug-fest, forever searching for cons to match every pro, finding anti-heroes or heroes to confront anti-heroes, seeking parallels of contradiction, the neat equation of opposites and forgetting that when you combine matter with anti-matter, you get nothing.

We always promote as much controversy as possible, looking behind every door for clashes between personalities like Ed Meese and Jim Baker, finding ways always for the inadvertent goof or offbeat remark.

We have a lot of these little habits like this that we take more or less for granted. Expressions of an adversary mind-set are as natural to us as subtlety and indirection are to the Chinese. Officials aren't enchanted but what is really worrisome is that a lot of readers and viewers aren't amused either. Journalistic practices claimed to be in the public interest are being questioned now by the public, as we can tell from polls, letters to the editor, and numerous other sources.

One reason is the egalitarian search which drove the events of the '60s and '70s intensified popular demands for fair and more equal treatment of the individual. The public apparently thought we should do the same thing. I think a perception that we have failed to live up to these heightened expectations largely accounts for the low esteem in which the press is now held by the public. This, in turn, contributes to the undermining of credibility.

Summing it all up, I believe the increasing adversarial nature of our society as a whole is deadlocking
the political process and menacing our ability to solve
the problems that threaten our prosperity and our
safety. Journalists can, and I believe should, play a
role in lowering the barriers that bar the kinds of consensus so critical to our democracy. In this cause, I
think that we can safely modify some of our more militant attitudes and adversarial practices without sur-
rendering ourselves to the political philistines or losing any of our vital organs. In other words, I don't
think we have to suffer any great loss of manhood as
we move somewhat in this direction.

HODGES: Thank you very much, Mike. Let's
turn next to Mike Gartner.

MICHAEL GARTNER: Last night Gene Patterson said Mike's speech to the ASNE was very brave
and very eloquent, and I certainly agree with that.
I thought so as I heard him deliver it. He had this
beautiful cadence, stentorian voice, and it wasn't until
I read it that I realized what he had said. It was a
lovely speech, but there was one thing wrong with it.
It addressed a problem that doesn't exist. He set up
a strawman and then knocked it down. Any editor
would have rejected it. Where were the names, where
were the places, where were the examples, where were
the dates, where were the anecdotes, the quotes, the
denials, the authorities?
   A regular complaint about the press is that we
write stories which the facts don't warrant. I don't
think the facts warranted what Mike said, although
he said it beautifully. He said, "The tendency in the
press has been to revel in the power and wield it freely
rather than to accept any corresponding increase in
responsibility." Who revels? Who doesn't accept
responsibility? Who among us is afraid to accept
responsibility?
   Mike says all newspapermen dream of being
movers and shakers; the thought that we may actually
be threatening the national government is inspira-

tional. Well, that's just hogwash. Newspapermen don't dream of being movers and shakers. It's a job. It's a job we like, we enjoy. Sometimes we're amazed that we get paid for doing it but we go home to kids and dogs and cars that don't work and washing machines that have leaked. We're not movers and shakers in the sense that you talk about. We just happen to have jobs that are very, very nice jobs.

He said, "No longer do we submit automatically to the rigors of old-fashioned impartiality. Not always but too often we surrender to the impulse of advocacy in the name of freedom, but forgetful of balance and fairness, and if it isn't too unfashionable to say so, what is good for the country."

That's marvelous language, but what is good for the country? Who knows what's good for the country? What's good for the country is truth and openness and aggressiveness and reporting what the news is. What is bad for the country is a press that becomes a handmaiden of government. Conspiratorial secrecy is what is bad for the country.

What is bad for the country is backroom deals, papers working hand-in-hand with the government. I think it's frightening that he would have editors think this is good for the country.

Later in this speech Mike says, "Adding to the general turmoil are two other phenomena: the press's harshly adversarial posture toward government and its infatuation with investigative reporting."

Setting aside the question of advocacy for the moment, I'm alarmed at your criticism of investigative reporting. I fail to see what's wrong with investigative reporting. People talk about Watergate as if it were a terrible sin of the press. We must remember, Watergate was the exposing of a terrible sin of the government, and it is not the press that should be on trial about Watergate. The government was on trial.

If you report that a mayoral candidate lied when he took the Fifth Amendment what is there to worry about? You shouldn't gloat about it but your reporters did their job. All good reporting is investigative reporting. We all worry about abuses and excesses but not in this context.

Later he quoted Roger Starr as saying muckraking did so much damage to the cities that he hated
to think what havoc modern investigative reporters
might commit. Again, what are the examples? What
have modern investigative reporters done to hurt life
in the cities? They've exposed the fact that children
in Harlem are eating paint and dying of lead poison-
ing. Is that bad? They're exposing cases of safety inspectors or housing inspectors or plumbing inspectors
on the take. Is that bad? There's pollution in the cities
and this is explored and discussed in the newspapers.
Is that bad? I just have a hard time grasping any of
these grand quotes because the examples would tend
to be just the opposite.

Later Mike says, "Similar questions need to be
asked about our intensely adversarial coverage of
government because this, too, is falsely coloring the
information flowing to the public."

Let me give you another quote from someone who
says, "There are the endless official lies and deceits
and masquerades that gnaw at the moral intent of
reporters." Well, you said that, too, Mike. That's a
quote I rather liked in this speech, so I cite that to
rebut your general thesis.

Gene Patterson, in his ASNE speech said, "The
adversary process must continue." Ben Bradlee, in an
interview in *American Heritage* magazine two months
ago said the one difference he has noted in
Washington over the years since he has been editor
of the *Post* is the increasing deception, the increasing lying of government officials to reporters. And so
I worry that if we worry about being adversaries the
deception will continue. The public, of course, will be
the loser.

In Mike's talk earlier today, he said, "We need
consensus and conciliation." I agree with that. But
the way we get to that is through the adversarial process. Just like in lawsuits, the way you get to consensus and conciliation is through the adversarial process. In classrooms, the way you get to consensus is
through the adversarial process. You explore all sides.

Now, adversarial doesn't mean nasty. It just
means exploring and taking positions. The press's

position is not a position of right or wrong but a position to print the truth. The government's position is a position to only disclose favorable facts. Once the public understands that, consensus and conciliation can be attained. There's nothing wrong with consensus and conciliation. I agree with him completely about that.

Later on in the speech, he says, "We should begin with an editorial philosophy that is more positive." My goodness, Mike, you sound like the chamber of commerce in Des Moines, not like the editor of the *Daily News.*

It is not the function of the press to be positive. It is not the function of the press to be negative. It is the function of the press to explore, to expound, to expand, to explain, to disclose as much as can humanly be disclosed.

We should be less arrogant, he says. And I agree, totally. I think every editor agrees we should be less arrogant. Editors should be less arrogant, reporters should be less arrogant, but that doesn't mean that we should become more positive.

We should make peace with the government, he says. We should not make peace with the government. We should not make peace with anyone. We should not be aligned with any segment of society, whether it's government or whether it's the school board or whether it's the chamber of commerce or whether it's the American Society of Newspaper Editors. We must be independent. And we cannot be independent if we have a policy of detente with any area we cover.

Mike says, "We should develop a more sensitive value system to be sure we do not needlessly hurt public figures while exaggerating the public's right to know. Legitimate public needs should be weighed against the personal harm because, among other things, the fear of media harassment is already seriously affecting recruitment for public service."

I just cannot accept that. I don't think you can exaggerate the public's need to know. Maybe not their *right* to know but their *need* to know. And I think that if persons are unwilling to stand the public scrutiny or the scrutiny of the press to take government service, then the government is better off without those persons.

Finally, Mike says, "Editors also need to be ruthless in ferreting out the subtle biases, cultural, visceral and ideological, that still slip into copy in political stories mostly, but also into the coverage of emotional issues like nuclear power and abortion."

I think he is absolutely right. I think the loaded word, the cheap shot, the insensitive choice of words or organizations are problems in the press. But I think the problems can be dealt with by an editor's pencil, not by a whole change in policy.

To sum up, Mike gave a brave and eloquent speech. I've heard it quoted endlessly by businessmen, by chambers of commerce, by lawyers in court. They all love it. It has only one serious flaw—it's simply wrong. Napoleon said, "I fear three newspapers more than 100,000 bayonets," and it's only too bad, Mike, that he never met you.

HODGES: All right. Thank you. And now we turn to Martin Linsky.

MARTIN LINSKY: I think you have to go back and ask what this First Amendment freedom of expression business is all about in terms of the relationship between press and government. And I think you'd agree, it has something to do with getting the truth out and something to do with getting the broadest number of people involved in the debate about public affairs. That's why we have it and that's why we value it.

What's changed? What's new? One of the consistent themes that ran through almost all the material sent us in advance was that the press has become a lot more powerful. I don't think anybody argues with that. The press has a different power relationship with government than existed 20 or 30 or 40 years ago.

The question, then, is what does this mean? What are the consequences? What should we think about the relationship? My problem is that although the press has this new power, which everybody seems to acknowledge, it seems to be playing by the old rules, the rules that were okay when it had a lot less power.

Now, there are serious consequences of that condition. A mistake made by the press, when the press was not all that important, didn't have that kind of leverage. It didn't have such great consequences. A mistake made by the press, or an abuse or excess, in conditions of great power has different consequences. It has more far-reaching consequences, more compelling consequences. It affects society more.

So what's wrong with that? We all know, we all accept the notion that there are going to be mistakes. But if you take the great power and then the mistakes, the public is going to be unhappy.

When banks abused their power, the public did something about that. When the railroads abused their power, the public did something about that. When any institution in our society has great power and abuses it, the public does something about it. And I think that's really what we're talking about here.

We're talking about a situation in which there is abuse of power or mistakes or excesses, the loss of public confidence, the loss of public credibility. The consequence of that is that society is going to do something about it.

To me, libel judgments are the tip of the iceberg. That is the way, the first way, that the public can get back.

Look at the Freedom of Information Act changes. Look at the secret agents' law and the reclassification system. Look at what states and the federal government are trying to do. Society will find a way. It's society that gave us the First Amendment. It didn't come from God, it came from people. And what society gives, society can take away. I think that's the risk and I think that's the issue.

I would not be surprised if I could come back here 150 years from now, to look on this debate as one which determined the state of First Amendment freedoms in this country for the next 50 to 75 years.

Now, the next question, it seems to me, is what is the relationship between the press and government?

I don't think we know very much about it. There has been a lot of anecdotal evidence but it seems to me it is not adversarial, it is not symbiotic, it is not independent, it is not under the tent. It's clearly a marble cake. It's a combination of all those things.

I have been on both sides of this fence and I understand it, sometimes. At 9 o'clock it's adversary, at 10 o'clock it's symbiotic. At 11 o'clock it's independent and at 12 o'clock the politicians are manipulating the press. It goes back and forth, it's all over the place. You can't say it's one or the other and try to do that. It's artificial.

To talk about real enemies, real adversaries, is silly. You're kidding yourself. Both say they're doing the people's business. And most of the time, what they're doing is their own business and each other's business. But they really do share perspective and a view.

Now, what are the really large problems I see in the relationship between press and government? They come, I think, from the condition that I described before: big power and the consequences of excesses or mistakes. When you have a lot of power as an institution or an industry, whether you're the banks or the journalists or government, I think you've got to begin to think of yourself in the whole course of history, not in the moment.

The issues are long-term, they're historic. They're decisions being made on the day-to-day battlefield, whether you fight a libel suit, you respond to "Jimmy's World," or run a gossip column in your newspaper. Those decisions are going to have short-term consequences. But they're going to have long-term consequences in whether the kind of freedom of the press we enjoy now is going to be maintained. Those are the building blocks of public credibility, the public attitude on which the First Amendment rests.

The words that come to my mind are *accountability, self-awareness, self-discipline, self-restraint* — things that mature people and mature institutions pride themselves on. I think about the word *sensitivity*. It's a word I've seen used a couple of times, but not very often. Sensitivity is a value that it seems to me ought to be introduced into this business. When I look at the Jimmy's World case, the thing that I can't get away from is why didn't Ben Bradlee say, "Let's find help for that kid.?" Why weren't people ripped up inside? What is it about the way we operate that says when you print a story about an eight-year-old heroin addict you don't make sure that you go find that kid and do something. I don't really understand that.

I think there has to be a sense of consequences. I can't disagree with Mike Gartner more on that point. Grown-up people, grown-up industries, responsible professionals have to accept responsibility for the logical consequences of what they do. It's not a momentary flight of imagination to say, when I print this article it's going to cause enormous pain and trouble for one person or one family for a little bit of public good. Am I doing the right thing or should I put a recipe in that place, or a letter to the editor or something else? You know as well as I do that we're always making decisions about what goes in and what goes out. So the question really is, is it worth the candle. Will that particular piece do more harm than good? You've got to think of that. You've got to take responsibility for the consequences. You're doing it.

Sometimes we don't know what the consequences are but I'm saying in most cases we do. It's not a question of Wernher von Braun just throwing the bombs up and letting them come down where they may. They're your bombs. You're creating them. You're a big force and you have to take responsibility for that.

The last one is *fairness.* It seems to me fairness is an important value. Fairness doesn't have anything to do with adversarialness. Just like accuracy doesn't have anything to do with adversarialness. You can be as adversarial as you want without being unfair, without being inaccurate.

Let me now run through what I see as the litany of small issues involved in the relationship between press and government. The first one, and maybe the overriding one that relates most directly to the adversary press, is that we are in the bad news business.

We don't put good news on the front page most of the time. And what are the consequences for government and public officials? I think the consequences are real and they're serious. They do undermine public confidence in individuals and government. But if you're going to have adversary journalism—and I hope adversary journalism continues to be the main thrust of relations between the press and government—it's got to be done in an environment in which you feel honestly that you are portraying in your newspaper a full picture. If you feel that telling that bad story, in an environment in which you create a total picture of government for people who read your paper, is honest, then that's okay. Government officials know that great hitters only bat .350, which means that most of the time they strike out. Government officials understand that. I don't think government officials are looking for a batting average of .700. They're looking for a batting average that reflects the environment in which they work. They understand that bad news is your business.

The second thing is gossip. Gossip journalism seems to me to be the worst underbelly of what we're talking about. It doesn't meet the standards of adversarialness, it doesn't meet the standards of fairness, it doesn't meet the standards of accuracy which we apply. And when it works in the government's business, it's particularly pernicious.

Privacy. We are in a world in which it is tough to keep personal privacy. It's not easy. All you've got is your reputation and personal privacy. Shouldn't we keep thinking about that? Whenever you write a piece that invades somebody's personal privacy, shouldn't you think about the consequences of what you're doing?

Agenda setting. I thought Mike Gartner's interview with Ben Bradlee in *American Heritage* was brilliant. It was brilliant because I think it made Ben Bradlee reveal much more than he intended to reveal. One of the things he did for the first time that I've seen was to say, "Sure, we set the national agenda." That's a big responsibility. How much can we think about that? How much can we take responsibility for doing that? I think journalists feel comfortable putting issues on the national agenda that the public officials don't put on the agenda. I don't think it's a big issue. I don't think it counts for very much. In fact, when it does count I think it's a good idea. That is, if the politicians aren't speaking about an issue, it seems to me it's the journalist's responsibility to get it out there. I've got no problem with that.

The anonymous source, to me, is one of the greatest little issues in this relationship between the press and government. One of the complaints you hear all the time from people in public service is, how can I deal with criticisms and comments about me personally and about my efforts from people I deal with all day if I don't know who they are? How many times have I seen in the *Boston Globe* stories about public officials where anonymous quotes are used only to make the story work—good, sexy quotes, criticism, harsh things that people wouldn't say if they had to be held accountable.

The last point is the use of motives. Once again, there's nothing wrong. In fact, it's terrific, to me, that we have journalism that tries to get at people's motives. But if we always come back, because of our point of view, to the fact that people in public life are self-interested and cynical then that's not quite a virtue to go around looking for people's motives. If we're really trying to define the source of decision making, why people do what they do, how they waive those alternatives and values in making their decision, that's something very different. But most of the motive-based stories that I see try to attribute everything said or done to self-interest.

That's really the end of my list. I think there's enormous room for taking this issue of the relationship between press and government, for analyzing and understanding it and for building on the groundwork that Mike Gartner and Mike O'Neill have made this morning.

GARTNER: I'd like to clarify the point about consequences. What I meant was that once the decision is made to print a story, I think editors should not worry about the consequences. The story should be printed based upon its news value, not on its consequences.

Now, in determining its news value, one might give more than fleeting attention to the potential consequences. But that should not be the overriding determination.

HODDING CARTER: I think my opening remark would have to be that while I wasn't an elected official, I was a public official for a while, so I share some of Marty's (Linsky) perspective. I have to say that that perspective does not allow me to accept either Michael O'Neill's notion of the press as grand inquisitor nor Michael Gartner's thesis of the press as the tribune of the people.

I'm more impressed, in fact, with the press in the relationship that I knew best in terms that were described by John Chancellor when we were sitting in Vienna getting ready to sign the SALT II agreement. It was late at night and he came to me and said, "How are my mates down there at the State Department these days." And I said, "They're fine." And he said, "You know, one of the real problems with those boys is they put on their team jacket with Henry Kissinger and they've never taken it off."

I think to a large degree a great part of the press, whether they think that they're playing grand inquisitor or whether they think they're playing hard ball newspapering, dance a very elaborate minuet with government. We're all dancing to music we know, the steps we understand, and which largely escape the understanding or the hearing of the public at large.

It is a continuing surprise to me to hear, given either indirectly with some modesty by representatives of the press or with panic by representatives of the public order, the notions of the great power that the press is supposed to be wielding independent of all other aspects of society.

If you all will tell me one major American problem which the press anticipated and set on the national agenda, as opposed to running behind and trying to catch up after it surfaced, I'll eat half of what I can remember. On the other hand, if you can tell me, including Watergate, one major consequential act in which the press fractured society, I'll be tremendously surprised.

I know we all like to bask either in the glow of Watergate or worry about its consequences but, as has been observed by better people than me, you know, it took one second rate judge and some leaked grand jury proceedings, not the work of two cub reporters, to bring the real consequences of that event about.

As a matter of fact, there is one thing that Marty said, among many things he said, with which I agree. There really is an overwhelming sense of contempt on the part of many public office holders toward the press. Not for reasons that you think. There is a continuing sense, by those who are involved in the direct manufacturing of the news, that the press daily flunks the test of accuracy and fairness and of understanding and of focus and of perspective and of any sense of continuity and of any notion that there are, in fact, issues which endure over time which are not easily resolved. And finally, they feel that the form you choose to present events inherently distorts them over and over again.

It is not a healthy business because we are, press and government, in this minuet. We are all, in fact, in many ways club members.

I would say that my assessment of the power of the press is distorted in one sense. There is no question that financially and because the press controls the pipeline, it is a powerful sort of institution.

That being so, one of the things I'm rather taken by is that it's usually only in seminars like this that we choose to confront each other in ways which are meaningful. There's no other institution in American society which we would so readily leave alone in our public commentary and in our coverage when dealing with its effects on society. This is a powerful

institution. But newspapers in 1,740 towns operate
totally without any kind of check from other
newspapers.

The least we might do is look across each other's
shoulders and say, "That one was a low blow. That
one was badly done. That was lousy coverage." The
public perception of the press is that it's not only
powerful but a closed club which very carefully makes
sure that when there's any attack on one, no matter
how egregious the error has been, the club closes
ranks and refuses to concede the error. The Union
Club has nothing on the press club. Nothing.

EUGENE PATTERSON: I would agree, Hodding, the press is a rival for the Union Club. We are
a pack, a herd. We are overly sensitive about the
regard of our peers.

We're afraid to speak out the way Mike O'Neill
did, normally. Why did it take so long for anybody
to say what he said? And as clearly and as plainly
as he said it. I salute him for doing that.

I think, Hodding, that you have raised some questions here. The minuet the press dances with government should be raised again in the seminar that Bill
Greider's book is triggering here a month from now.
He feels, as you do, that somehow the public is not
being served by the system of coverage in Washington.
He argues that we're covering things on each other's
terms, the press and the government. And that needs
exploring.

I want to go back to Marty Linsky and Mike Gartner and suggest that I disagree with them on one principal pillar of their arguments. Marty said fairness
doesn't have anything to do with adversarialness. I
think it does. I think the very nature of the adversary system is to be unfair.

You say we get to consensus and conciliation
through the adversary process. I just can't picture a
prosecutor and defense attorney standing in front of
a jury seeking consensus and conciliation. They're
seeking advantage for their client.

GARTNER: You're confusing adversary with advocacy.

PATTERSON: No, I'm confusing it with what I perceive to be the adversary system, which is what lawyers practice. Therefore, if the press practices the adversary system, are we not reducing the role we play in society? Are we not lowering the level of our elevated position as a stater of facts, to contenders, political claimants?

You said that the way to conciliation and consensus is through the adversary process, and I cannot see that as being true. You say that fairness doesn't have anything to do with adversarialness, and I think adversarialness is based on unfairness. Present the facts in the way to make your case the most clearly and reduce the effectiveness of the other man's argument. Is that what the press is about?

LINSKY: I think it would be skepticism as opposed to neutrality.

HODGES: Adversarialness is based on skepticism?

LINSKY: The questioning skepticism, the doubt, the presumption. I think those are mind-sets and attitudes that don't have to produce unfair journalism.

So if we get to the adversary system, it seems to me we're loading the deck against the press and giving up the very high ground of fairness as I perceive it. I think we're giving that up and reducing ourselves to a level below the point on the ladder where we should be.

GARTNER: By adversary, I mean the press isn't necessarily itself the adversary. If you're doing something in government, you seek out the adversary, the other side. That is how the public achieves consensus.

O'NEILL: I think the American Anglo-Saxon legalistic approach is that every issue has to be a contest. When one idea battles against another idea, we arrive at the truth. I'm saying that's a lot of hogwash. We may arrive at the truth or we may not arrive at the truth. If every individual has to have opposition in order for the adversary process to work, then you help generate and create opposition when the opposition may not actually be there.

HODGES: Let's turn to Art Caplan and see if he wants to deal with the issue of the nature of adversarialness.

ARTHUR CAPLAN: It seems to me that there really is an argument here about what ethos should dominate reporting or doing journalistic work.

I don't see any connection between adversarialness and truth. The point of adversarialness, in the two contexts where it is the ethos, law and politics, is never truth. It is justice. That's what people expect from an adversarial system. That is why fairness is absolutely linked to adversarialness. There's no break in between because fairness refers to procedure, justice of procedure, in the adversarial process.

We do have other professions that make truth their ethos. For example, natural science is one area where professionals have a certain set of values: openness, duplication, sharing, testing, appeal to commonly agreed upon methods, appeal to commonly agreed upon systems of measurement and technique. Those are the values that guide scientists in the pursuit of what? Truth, not justice. If one wants to pursue truth, one starts to think that if that's the goal for journalism, adversarialness has very little to do with truth. I don't think we have to go that far because there's room to do both. But one starts to realize there are different methods and techniques and approaches to values one might have depending on whether one selects the truth as the goal of the enterprise, or justice, or some others that haven't been mentioned yet—entertainment, profit, understanding, consensus. All of those have different values that will adhere to the procedures and methods appropriate to them.

Think about the humanities for a second—what a boring moment—but let's think about them anyway. One thing that we do in the humanities is to state our values up front. We're not ashamed of bias. It's the real-reasoned defense of values that determines what we consider the truth.

In certain areas of life, when one is seeking coherence, when one is trying to build a well-argued position, one might say, "Here are my values, this is why I hold them. I'm going to try and move you toward seeing values in my way." So there are certain areas of inquiry in which values are going to be stated and defended, and they are not incompatible with talking about truth.

So I make the following point, to recap what I said. It seems to me that adversarialness is something quite different from the methods and techniques that we commonly associate with seeking the truth. I think we get too caught up in the operation of journalism. We may, in fact, not be able to see the forest for the trees. There are lots of different fields, endeavors, activities out there where people pursue different ends and adversarialness is only one of them.

I'd agree to believe it only pursues one key value, justice. Whether that's the appropriate one, the only value that ought to guide journalistic behavior, I don't know. But I think there are different approaches to the truth and when we start to talk about seeking out opponents or adversaries on positions, we're getting over to that truth model.

That's very different from adversarialness. What value should the journalistic profession pursue and is there only one? If there's a multiplicity, maybe different people within the profession will have to have different values and therefore, different modes appropriate to their pursuit.

HAROLD EVANS: What might be useful at this stage is to think of the Anglo-Saxon system of justice and the continental system of justice. The Anglo-Saxon system assumes that two advocates will clash and produce justice, not the truth. I've heard many

a judge in Anglo-Saxon courts say we're not here seeking the truth, we're here to seek a settlement or
resolution or conciliation, if you like. But if you go
to a French court, the prosecuting magistrate tries
to see what the truth is.

JAMES HOGE: As far as Mike O'Neill's piece
is concerned, I don't take issue with it because he has
concerns. Indeed, I share some of his concerns. I don't
take issue with the fact that he asks us to really examine some of our attitudes and practices.

But I do end up taking great issue with the speech
because I think it does, indeed, set up a strawman.
I think it does, indeed, get wholly out of proportion
on several very key issues. Take the issue of power.
We have to look at that in a relative sense. If the units
of the press are larger, and therefore more powerful,
what about the rest of society? What about government responsibilities? What about private enterprise?

Most of your units of power or concentrations of
power are a great deal larger and therefore the relationship between them may not be that much different
than it has always been. Indeed, there's been an
awesome growth in the ability to manipulate communication within government, not within the press.
There is no comparison between increases in public
relations budgets of the Pentagon over a quarter of
a century and the internal budgets of our newspapers.

Mike, it seems to me, really tipped his hand this
morning when he said his real concern is the crisis
facing the nation. Those are his words, not mine. And
I think he has gotten out of proportion. Where, indeed,
are our crises coming from? Are they coming from objective things that have happened here or are they
coming from the way things are being reported on,
examined and explored?

Now, for every one of his major points, he could
make a devil's advocate argument. Society is not functioning. All right, we know it's got some very difficult
problems but you could turn that right on its head
and say —

O'NEILL: I didn't blame the press for any of this. Get it accurate.

HOGE: I know you didn't. I'm leading up to what you had to say about the press. I think there's an important point to be made. Society is not functioning, you said. There are very many problems. All right, we've got lots of problems we could talk about, about the way Congress works, state houses work, and so on, but we do see examples of anything but paralysis.

Lastly, let's look at the remark that adversarial culture is debilitating. That's the one I'd really like to concentrate on. I'll overstate the case against it. I think you can take the counter position that a society in which the contentions and tensions are observable is a more healthy society than one in which that is not the case.

A sociologist named Frank Tannenbaum wrote about ten years ago that a society in which the tensions are not observable and therefore cannot be dealt with is a dead society. It is either part of antiquity or it is under some form of authoritarian control.

I think that this is particularly necessary in a society like ours, which is so pluralistic, which is so reasonably diverse, which is so large. I think the real need is not necessarily to find some way of living without contention, without observable social tension. The real need is to make sure we maintain a process that allows for and sometimes fosters the changes and the alterations that have to be made to address those tensions as they come up.

That is where the focus should be—that we are still more successful than unsuccessful as a society in dealing with such things. If, indeed, we're now in a period of time of less argumentativeness or lowered social tensions than we were in the '60s and '70s, I would maintain that, in part, it's because exhaustion follows great activity. But I would also say, let us not overlook that it is because there have been some very fundamental changes. We did, indeed, have a civil rights revolution in this country. However imperfect our racial relations remain, that is an historic development that very few societies can point to.

We have had a woman's movement which, despite a recession, has now proved that it has become a fundamental part of the fabric of this country. We did, indeed, end the colonial war that was debilitating the country. We could go on, I think. There are other things we could point to.

So I think that adversarialness or contentiousness is not the issue. Indeed that may be a sign of health. An issue could be, do we have a system which allows for some remedial activity? Not perfection. I don't know if we get as far in the next round of challenges. I know my argument would be that we do.

HODGES: Let's turn to Harry Evans and see where he wants to take us.

EVANS: I'd like to take issue with Mike Gartner on one point and make a general point about the sort of terms we're using.

Taking issue with Mike first. I think it's wrong to think only of taking consequences of ethical by-play or the marginal factor. I found in my time as an editor that taking consequences was, in fact, one of the only ways to make judgments about what you call news values. I don't know how you can make a news value or a news judgment without thinking in a wider context.

Why is something news? Why is a tornado news? Why is something else news? Because it has consequences to people. You can't rule out consequences.

GARTNER: Are you talking about consequences to society or consequences to the person you're writing about?

EVANS: I don't think that news judgments can begin at all without some kind of value judgment. There's no such thing as news unless you've got a value judgment there before it. And that's where I take issue when you say, oh, well, there's news value and then marginally there may be a thing called consequences. There's not. They're all the same thing. Otherwise, how can you find your way through the plethora of bits of information? What's relevant? Why is it relevant? It's relevant because it affects people's lives and happiness.

So you're placing a value on ethical judgments, you're disguising it as a kind of hard-boiled, professional, hairy-chestedness, which isn't really put there.

GARTNER: I don't think that's the issue. The issue was the consequence to the individual involved, Secretary Donovan, for instance or Richard Allen. It wasn't the consequence to society.

EVANS: Ah, well, wait a minute. An individual's in society. The consequence to an individual is as relevant as the consequence to that mass which is made up of individuals.

GARTNER: Are you saying, then, they shouldn't have written the Richard Allen stories because, after all, it screwed up his life.

EVANS: No, don't get me wrong. I'm not saying what the judgment would be in a particular case. In my judgment, circumstances determine everything. And there's no absolute thing like a news value that determines it.

GARTNER: You're talking about impact on society as a whole, and I don't disagree with you. But I was talking about the consequence on the individual person involved in the story when you're writing that. And what I say is that that is not of momentous concern. Once you've made the decision to print the story you no longer are concerned about consequences.

GAYE TUCHMAN: One of the things that strikes me, not being a member of this particular club and recognizing that you all are indeed members of a club of some power, is that all of a sudden, some very powerful members of this very powerful estate are saying, "My God, what happened? We have power."

There's some kind of contradiction here that I find fascinating, especially because I suspect that this power has not arisen in the past 10 or 15 years. It has been there for some time, and I don't quite understand why you're all not willing to recognize that.

I wanted to say something, Hodding, specifically to your example of naming one thing that the media put on the national agenda.

People have been batting about Watergate in terms of what it is that the media did or did not do. And it's been batted about as though it were all of a piece. But those of you who were covering Watergate at the time know that it wasn't all of a piece. It was a very long, extended process that had twists and curves and moments when Watergate meant one series of incidents and moments when it meant another series of incidents; moments when all of a sudden the people who create the *New York Times* index decided there was a phenomenon called Watergate that they could put in the index. Before that, they didn't even know what it was.

That, in part, is a question or response to your request for something the media anticipated. That process involved bits and pieces of give and take that the media sometimes anticipated.

I want to say a couple of other things, also, that have to do with this notion of adversarial relationships.

I recently read an admiring biography of Phyllis Schlafly by a feminist. One of the things that she discussed was the ways the media helped create Schlafly not merely by going to her and finding a second side, but also because the reporters who were sent to talk with Schlafly never knew enough about the ERA to be able to tell whether Schlafly was telling the truth. That is a serious accusation which goes well beyond the question of the prize-fight school of journalism.

C. K. McCLATCHY: Before I get to the substance of Mike O'Neill's talk, I just wanted to get away from some of these more cosmic things to a couple of generalizations that I think both Mikes, in a different manner, got to concerning newsmen.

When Mike O'Neill talks about some newsmen revelling in power and being arrogant and when Mike Gartner says he doesn't know any, I think we really have to keep in mind we're talking about individuals. I don't think either one of those generalizations will hold up. I think that newsmen are like plumbers or any other people.

In our particular group, we're not exempt from having individuals who have special quirks. And I suspect that you could find that there are significant differences between say, Bill Thomas and Ben Bradlee.

WILLIAM THOMAS: You'd better believe it.

McCLATCHY: I'm not sure this is very important but I think we've got to keep in mind that you can't generalize about people in our business.

And going to the more important thing, which is the substance of what Mike O'Neill said, I think he has touched on some important things we ought to deal with. But I think when you get down to the essence of what Mike said he was talking about being more conscious of what is good for the country, and trying to understand how things will affect the country.

In that area I agree with Mike Gartner. I don't think we can do our job if we spend a lot of conscious effort sorting out ahead of time what is going to be good or bad for the country. It may be very simplistic but I think if we simply do our job of reporting the news as well as we can, we're doing the best we can for the country. I don't think we ought to do a lot more.

JAMES BATTEN: It seems to me as we go through this discussion that we have to remember that there is enormous accumulated evidence out there that people don't like us. They don't respect us.

Marty, you hit on that when you talked about libel cases being the tip of the iceberg and that what society has given, society can take away. I'm personally concerned about that. All survey evidence I see says that if people have a chance to punish us, if they ever get into a position to punish us, they're going to punish us.

I was involved the other day in an ANPA committee meeting that was the beginning of a very interesting and maybe dangerous debate about First Amendment protection for the electronic media. As electronics and print converge there's the danger that the broadcast model rather than the print model will be extended.

The thing that concerns me is that some people who have a sort of macho First Amendment flavor about them say that obviously the electronic media ought to have the same protection print has traditionally had. Substantively, I don't disagree with that.

I'm worried that if we wind up having a First Amendment debate in this country right now, as a part of trying to deal with the electronic media, we might wind up losing a lot because the debate would be in the context of a period when we're out of favor.

It seems to me that if Mike is wrong, and I personally don't think he's wrong in any large respect, we all have the obligation to figure out what the problem is. We do not have a little problem, we have a great big problem. And unless we fix it, we may all lose something that is extremely precious to us.

ROY PETER CLARK: My wife and I play this little game. It's called the vulture game. We count the number of times newsmen are represented as vultures on television and in movies. Any time they are, they're always attacking someone. They appear in groups, in packs of vultures to pick the bones of various people clean.

I'm wondering if that's not, in part, due to not only the relationship of the press to government and its attitude towards government but to the way the press deals with other sorts of citizens and other sorts of situations.

When Air Florida Flight 90 crashed in Washington, that plane was headed for Tampa. And there was something which became known as the "death watch" at the Tampa airport, where the people waiting for those people to come on Flight 90 sat in a little lounge. Their comments were that the one great horror of that evening was the way the press treated them rather than the fact that they lost a loved one.

Recently, the *St. Petersburg Times* ran a story about a black man who is a murderer, who had come from a black neighborhood named Methodist Town. That town was described as something like a sewer of violence, drugs, murders, rapes and unwed mothers. I grew up in lower East Side New York, and I suppose the description would have fit the place I grew up, except that my mother lived there.

So in the same way, many people who are law-abiding, God-fearing, respectable people who had grown up in that community objected. I don't think we can ever overestimate what it means to be in the newspaper, to have your name or something you know about mentioned in the newspaper.

Let me give one more example of someone who is a public figure. There was a story on John Hinckley in *Rolling Stone* magazine. At the end of this article the reporter speculates on what would conceivably happen if Hinckley were to get out of jail. And he has this sort of fantasy scene in which Hinckley gets out of jail and eventually calls his father and says, "Hello, Dad, this is John. I just shot Jodi Foster. Can I come home?"

In the next issue of *Rolling Stone* there was a letter from Foster, which I hope you all have the chance to read sometime, in which she says, "How could you trade my life so cheaply for a cute ending to your story?"

I guess what I'm saying is that people, both in the public eye and including some of you, who are written about all the time, do have firsthand knowledge of events. It's easy to get outraged, based on press misbehavior. And I think a lot of that has to do with people who don't understand what it means to have your name in the paper or have your town written about in the newspaper. People read those things every day and they object to them. They're the ones who I think are going to be involved in making some of the final decisions as to what happens to the press in our society.

B. J. PHILLIPS: I think we're really in deep stuff out there with the folks. And I think in a way we ought to start trying to figure out how we got there.

I think what's happened is that we have created television newspapers and television news magazines. We have started increasingly to cover not only those things which television covers, but to cover them in the same way that television covers them. Which gets us to this entire adversarial thing.

Because television only has 45 seconds on a given story, the quickest and cheapest, and certainly the most efficacious way to get at the story is to set up two opposing quotes. We all know that the truth is not necessarily the square root of two diametrically opposed quotes. And yet on an expanded basis we do that same thing, with far less excuse.

They are the originators of the glaring ambush journalism that resulted in the assaults on these people in the Tampa airport. We follow their techniques and we follow their ethical values which are shaped by the necessity to get it live, get it on camera.

KATHERINE FANNING: I think B.J. raises a terribly important point. I know we're going to come back to it. Television is setting the agenda. But I just wanted to say I think Mike O'Neill has performed a tremendous service, whether he's right or wrong and I think he's part right and part wrong, by simply beginning this discourse. I think it's true that the increased power of the press, gained over the recent years, means increased responsibility.

But who are we accountable to? We're accountable to the public. And I think the public is speaking loud and clear when they say that we have no credibility, when they say that we are not fair, that we're not honest.

I think, too, we need to make a major distinction between the national press and those of us out in the boondocks. The young reporter who comes to work in someplace like Alaska is looking toward the national press, looking toward the *Washington Post,* the *New York Times,* the television reporters, and so forth. But at the same time, the power isn't anything like what the national press seems to enjoy.

It seems to me in this matter of the adversaries that what we should be talking about is degree and intensity. Of course we're going to question, we must question what government does, what power centers do. But do we have to do it with a kind of swarm psychology? I think we have to ask ourselves are we involved in public service or self service?

If it's self service, it's what competition does. We have to get it first. Sometimes, it seems to me, we have a big story that's about to break and we can get a leak from the grand jury or we can wait until the grand jury indicts. What is the public service in taking a leak from the grand jury two days before the indictment is going to come down, anyway? The main objective in doing that is just to beat the competition. Is that always a worthy goal? I think we need to look at that.

On the Donovan question and others like it, I think when we publish a story like that, which I think we have a duty to do, we need to ask ourselves what if we're wrong about this? Maybe he isn't guilty. And yet we absolutely surround the story and we give it tremendous prominence and we beat it and beat it and beat it without ever stopping to say, maybe we're destroying someone unfairly, unjustifiably.

These are some of the questions I'm really glad to see us discussing. And I think that if we don't hit them head on, we are going to lose our credibility, we are going to be considered untruthful and irresponsible, as much of the public considers us now.

THOMAS: I just wanted to say that halfway through this entire thing, it just struck me we're just talking about whether we handle stories professionally or we don't handle them professionally. That's the essence of it. A myriad of factors go into the judgment of every single story, all of the things we've talked about. We talk about being unpopular today. We've always been unpopular. By some standards, we're even a little more popular today than we were, say in the '30s.

Hodding said that the politicians look upon us with some contempt, probably because of what they perceive as our lack of expertise and our lack of commitment to accuracy. The same thing is true of sports figures, entertainment figures and corporate executives. It's true of anyone with a particular view of the world. And quite often, probably, they're right. But quite often, too, they're reflecting a peculiar view of their own which perceives accuracy only from their own vantage point. I just don't see any way, despite how we agonize, that we can ever back off from our basic responsibility, which is to one way or another get the important information before the people who have to see it. That doesn't mean we shouldn't treat people with civility in all cases, if possible. It doesn't mean we can't be humane, it doesn't mean we crucify people without good reason. But it means we still have to pursue that one, main objective, I think.

As for television setting the agenda, I seem to see a different trend. Those newspapers which have improved, and quite a few have, are going the other way from the TV agenda. They're filling gaps that TV leaves, by being more thoughtful.

CARTER: The basic task is, indeed, the business of getting information across accurately. And I have to say to you now, going back to my old hat, that the contempt had better not be disregarded.

And finally, a personal note. Until I gave a speech in Rochester, New York, four months ago, I had never been interviewed by a reporter in my life in which there was not at least one, basic, factual error. Not some notion of nuance, not someone trying to read my head, which is perfectly legitimate. I mean just factual.

And I was always reminded of the reporters who would come rolling in to see George Wallace, and get their brains beaten in. You know why? Because they didn't know enough to deal with him, and the average reporter, coming to cover the things reporters cover, came unprepared to deal with him. So they were had.

It is the factual problem that is going to finally kill us. I think people out there want us to be adversaries. But they want us to be right. And if we had a lot less emphasis on being prophets, anticipating history, and a lot more emphasis on being right, there'd be a lot stronger feeling about our own standing today.

TUCHMAN: There is empirical stuff out on this question that Hodding was talking about. And I think that everything Hodding said is absolutely correct, when it comes to the relationships between reporters and their sources and the government officials. But it doesn't work that way with regular people, whom everyone likes to call the public. Instead, what tends to happen is that the guy who was in the automobile accident knows that his story was reported incorrectly, but when it comes to a truly big issue, something this person could not know directly about, he goes back to trusting the media. There's more of a tendency to be critical about what you know and to simply accept statements made about world affairs, about what's happening in Europe, about what's happening in Washington.

Has Television Changed the Rules?

OPENING STATEMENTS BY:

Hodding Carter
James Hoge

HODDING CARTER: You don't have to worry about me dealing with 15 minutes because the thing television teaches you is that you can tell everything you need to say in 20 seconds or 45 seconds or a minute.

To suggest that television has had some profound effects on the relationship between government and the media would be a mistake. If it suggests to you that now, because of television, government does things differently, that policy is somehow shaped in different ways, that it comes to different conclusions because television exists, that's one of the myths of the power of the press.

Television has a profound effect upon the way policy is presented and in ways that policy is planned for presentation. The first reason is, I think, best expressed in what a mutual friend and acquaintance of a number of us once said to me after he had left the South, covering the civil rights wars, and had gone to California to cover that state. I went out to visit him and he said, "Hodding, one thing you have to understand about this governor out here is that he's made us, in many ways, simply superfluous. We throw him our toughest questions and he looks right over our heads, talks into that lens and gets that message across no matter what the hell we do. He was speaking about Reagan, which I found amusing and preposterous at the time. I no longer find it very amusing or preposterous.

But it says something about what television does mean to government and to the relationship between government and people. In large measure, television becomes the all-important conduit for government to set the agenda on its own terms.

I want you to think with me how totally and completely government has been able to seize the high ground in policy debate and maintain it by simply using television in a regular, intelligent and planned way.

The most popular thing I know is for former government officials and present government officials to complain about the distorting effect of television, about its superficiality, about its inability to put things in context, its lack of memory and all the rest.

The dirty secret, from the government side, is that these are all assets for the government's presentation and the government's ability to do things. For instance, what is it we're supposed to do about the charts being used by the president in his news conferences. Television automatically means that the most you can do is have somebody say, in one balanced response, that that chart leaves something out.

What television can't do is to have a piece which essentially says this is full of baloney. How is it that at the end of a significant discussion of our policy initiative, television feels it necessary to have David Gergen or somebody else talking through one more time the administration's position in a long-term analysis?

Now, having said that television is in many ways an extraordinary tool for government, let me also say that if the screw turns in a different direction it becomes a significant problem. George Reedy said in one of his books that no president ever has a press problem, he has political problems. But presidents, being human, are never able to admit that they have political problems so they conceive of having press problems.

That's a backward way of getting into what I want to say on this point, which is that the government does not suddenly find itself attacked by a baying press. The government is finally attacked by political forces which have regathered on the outside, by a changing national consensus which disagrees with what the government is doing.

At that point that rather unfiltered lens through which the government's message has been thrown out begins to do more than simply carry the message. It begins, for the first time, to do what no administration wants, which is to act as a mirror to the other messages which have now gathered force.

It is then a problem for government that television is precisely what it is, except now in reverse. The forces gathered in opposition to the administration were not created by you folks or by television, but by the natural reaction of forces to what is being done. It is now impossible for the government to call off that particular dog.

Ronald Reagan didn't get a free hand for almost two years because the press was all that docile and because television was simply out there dealing with a great communicator, although that was important, as I suggested at the first. He also got a free run because the forces of opposition were fractured, disintegrated, and practically nonexistent at first. Only recently have they been able to articulate any kind of coherent opposition view. In the kind of America in which we live today this is another asset which government has in dealing with the press.

If you can think of any exceptional work that television has ever done in terms of the power relationships between media and government, tell me what it was. That is, what extraordinary series of work was done to illuminate some basic flaw in government or in policy. I think the answer is, if you find them, the exceptions will prove what I think is the rule.

The Iranian hostage crisis is frequently cited as an example, but let me tell you we turned that off and on whenever we wanted to. Remember this, for over two weeks we closed that thing down when Hamilton Jordan was running around in red wigs. I simply ceased to talk from the podium, and the story got lower and lower and lower. Somebody ought to do a study sometime. Because government did not choose to keep that up as a major story, it was simply tapped down to the point that it wasn't there.

Somebody mentioned poor old Jim Baker and Ed Meese and their supposed "dispute." Well, you know that story emerged because poor old Jim Baker and Ed Meese went rushing off into corners with various reporters, turning the tap up on it for their own reasons. It didn't come floating through by osmosis to brave reporters standing in the shrubbery outside the west wing of the White House. It was there because those guys chose to let it come through one of their folks.

JAMES HOGE: There's lots of research around, and it's growing, that says people may think television is their main source of news, but actually two-thirds of the American adult population gets the news from newspapers.

Look at how they watch television news. First of all, it's infrequent. Only a small band tunes in to see Dan Rather every night. The greater number are there out of habit or they're there because of the show before. They look at Dan Rather one night and somebody else the next. When you do watch, the most common activity is to make sure you're doing something else. You're reading, you're talking, you're picking up the apartment, whatever. And when you get through watching the news you can't remember what you watched. You cannot separate one item from another.

So yes, you can turn the news taps up or you can turn them down. But I think a very important thing to remember is that maybe the long-term effect either way, was really very inconsequential.

Television news in particular, it seems to me, shapes general *feelings* much more than it does *ideas*. In fact, I think Al Weston's comment as to how he conceived of his audience is really the key to it. He said the viewers tune in the news to assess how safe they are and how secure the world is. The rest of the details they are perfectly happy to have go in one ear and out the other.

That is a rather passive phenomenon which really can't do much in terms of agenda setting or governing. It reminds me of some political advice that was given by a very old and sage politician to Dan Walker, who had just won election as governor of Illinois. He had won it, coming from nowhere, with a phenomenal media campaign on television.

The advice given to him was, Dan, now that you're elected, please remember that television can get you elected, but you need the print medium to govern.

All those people out there have suddenly become con-
stituencies that overlap, that have much more defined
interests, and you need the newspapers to get at them
over time if you are to govern.

He was talking about television in the large context, television as a social phenomenon. There, it
seems to me, we have a more unmanageable beast.

There is a piece of new research which concludes
that those who watch a lot of television, and about
30 percent of the American public watch four hours
or more a day, have a grossly distorted view of the
real world. Among some of the characteristics of the
world they accept: We still live in a society
predominantly male-oriented, everything important
is done by males; there is no such thing as the
woman's movement; old people, for the most part, are
silly and feeble; minorities are inferior in all ways;
and the American population is disproportionately
made up of lawyers, doctors, athletes and entertainers.
Something that I found particularly ominous was that
their view of human life and of our society is one that
is far more violence prone and crime-ridden than it
actually is.

I mention this because it seems to me that that
is the world in which television news has to be considered, because it's the world in which it operates.

A word or two about bad characteristics of broadcast journalists viewed from the world of print. I would
submit that none of these characteristics necessarily
started with television. Indeed, many of them started
with us. We just don't like the way we see them as
they come back in a different medium, and I think
this is a legitimate way to play critic.

The first one is the thematic short story construction that dominates so much of what is called news
in television. There has to be a beginning, a middle,
and an end. There has to be a theme. There have to
be good guys and bad guys and it has to be resolved
right there in front of you. An extraordinary amount
of information which is useful to the general public
really cannot be constructed in a meaningful way
under such a format.

Then there's the fixation on mayhem, particularly on local news shows. It's not just that I think this
provides an inaccurate picture of the world or that
it gives us the idea that every other car is in an accident and every other person will be mugged, it is what
is *not* there.

As for the effect on newspapers, I'm particularly
worried about the trend toward brevity, capsulization,
color, statistics, and featurizing as ends in themselves
rather than as quite legitimate aids in communicating
information.

I do think we at least ought to think a good deal
about some of the problems of policy making and
policy execution in the world of the fishbowl, in the
world in which everything is instantaneous and in
which news is out before it's confirmed. Now, I want
to say very quickly I don't think the answer to that
problem is necessarily muddying up the water in the
fishbowl. Indeed, I don't think it's just a press problem or a television problem. It's a problem for public
officials to think about and react to, as well.

To give you just one example, George Shultz, who
is now secretary of state, is a man who's very concerned about these problems. And to my mind he's shown
a certain adeptness at controlling the fishbowl aspects
of policy making and policy execution. So I do think
there are some remedies.

The last effect I want to point to involves the
general public. This one I find particularly unsettling.
It is the tendency of television to create a sense of
distance between the public and the world in public
affairs. It tends to leave the public thinking that what
they are seeing is theater in which there are trained
players and celebrities but that they are not part of
it. That leads to alienation, to passivity, to lots of
things that we think are injurious in a democratic
society.

I started out by saying I think we exaggerate the
role of TV as an agenda-setter and I would submit
that, at most, TV sets a very superficial agenda.

What we all know is that the great trends in our
society, and that is the most significant agenda, occur

outside the world of politics. They occur outside the world of the press, and both politics and press eventually reflect those changes.

Secondly, there's a great deal of difference between agenda-setting and effectively governing. Again, I would submit that we have exaggerated mightily either the positive or the negative effects of television in terms of governing. The greater problems of the last 20 years have included a president who took us into a colonial war and started the Great Society at the same time, topping it all with the most massive deceitful public information policy that we've seen. He was followed by Richard Nixon and there we are.

My final point. I think there's a real message to those of us in the print media. The newspaper business is, indeed, in transition. Fourteen papers have died in the last two years. We've also had 25 papers started. There are all sorts of indices that point to health as well as to some sickness in the newspaper business. We too often overlook the fact that some problems result from inadequate management and from very major changes in our society and lifestyle. Where people live and how they live have made parts of our 1,740 newspapers no longer relevant, but not the body of the work we do.

If that's the case, then we have an obligation to make sure we remain the main source of information about what's occurring as well as why it's occurring. We don't just have an obligation, there is a need out there, and we're still the ones who are called upon to fill it.

CARTER: I don't have any great disagreement with the main thrust of anything Jim has said. But it hardly matters about the shifting nature of the television audience, and it hardly matters about the world view of that audience. The fact is, whatever the nature of the audience, it is the largest audience that any politician is going to have at any given time. For government it is the only way a policy is going to get an unfiltered run in whatever limited a way. I notice that one of the studies showed that only 50 million people see the evening news and that audience shifts all the time from channel to channel.

But if you're the president of the United States or you're a spokesman for the secretary of state you don't give a damn whether the audience is shifting between ABC, NBC, and CBS or CNN. All you care is that 50 million people are going to get your message.

KATHERINE FANNING: I think we're leaving out the emotional impact of television news completely. No one can tell me that the emotional impact of the pictures of the massacre in Lebanon didn't have an effect on U.S. public opinion which, in turn, had an effect on government.

CARTER: You are saying to me now that because of the emotional impact of those images on the American public opinion our government did what? Did it cut off aid to Israel?

ARTHUR CAPLAN: There comes a time in the discussion when you're looking at things from the moral point of view. You want to step back and say, let's not sully these arguments with facts.

Maybe the TV system can't do much, maybe it can. But what I'd like to see us talk a little bit about is what it should do.

I was thinking of one issue where I'm pretty sure the media created an issue. It's the creationism issue, and teaching it in the public schools. I think journalists cared about it, recognized it as a fundamental clash of rights. These little groups came along saying we're going to sue here, we're going to sue there. And it was made into an issue because there were people in the press who found it an interesting clash of values.

I can think of another issue that people keep disseminating information about and have the spigot wide open, but nobody in the press touches it. That is the whole issue of the increasing cost of health care. Media people don't know what to make of it. They can't understand it because it's complicated, it's technical, it's long-term, it's bizarre, and it's particularly difficult to get across on television. So the spigot is open and nobody seems to be bringing a bucket.

CARTER: May I say something peripherally on the creationism issue because this goes back to exactly what I'm talking about. In 1977, I sent my chief deputy down to Lynchburg, Virginia, to talk to Jerry Falwell about helping us sell the Panama Canal. I say that because it was pretty clear that Falwell wasn't one of six kooks sitting around in some corner, but somebody who reflected a power center which, quite frankly, a great part of the press had simply ignored.

Now the fact that the press came to the creationist story merely means that it was finally catching up with a story. The creationist movement was one which existed independently of any kind of mainstream press attention for a long time. Politicians knew it before you knew it. And then, finally, the press got it. And as usual, once coming upon something, it went completely berserk. But at least it was a real thing there.

ROY PETER CLARK: I wonder whether we might not be interested in discussing the way television news programs get the attention of viewers, the ways that they seek to put emphasis on news. What I'm saying is that lately we've been seeing, in stories about the economy and unemployment, television going out and seeking an unemployed worker in a very human and dramatic situation. You see an unemployed worker crying before you, while you're eating dinner. That has its effect on you. This also brings up the question of television news as entertainment and how that has perhaps affected us. As someone who teaches writing to journalists I always encourage students to seek out interesting and revealing anecdotes. I now wonder, as a result of watching television, whether that's not a dangerous thing. We pick out an anecdote, a story about an unemployed blue collar worker or someone else and, yes, it's dramatic. It captures your attention. But how truly representative is it of events as we come to know them?

One of the things that concerns me is what I would describe as the illusory nature of television news. We always assume that because these are pictures they are accurate descriptions of the real world. When I was at Auburn University I had the opportunity to be interviewed on television a few times in different ways. And I was shocked to find how make-believe the pictures that we saw really were. In one case I had written an article and was interviewed on the *Today* show. It was taped about six weeks in advance. Yet when they showed it on the *Today* show, they said, "Now from our studio in Washington is this interview," and they portrayed it as if it were a live interview. I was in Montgomery, Alabama, watching it. And somebody saw me at lunch at McDonald's and said, "How did you get back here so quickly?"

In another instance someone—a young reporter from Tuscaloosa, Alabama, interviewed me and then asked me to hold the camera while he asked the questions, and it was all spliced together. It came out nicely. No matter where the news occurs in Washington, the reporter rushes to the front lawn of the White House. I understand there's one really good angle from where all those pictures are taken. So here we are, it's live, you're seeing it now. And I'm wondering, isn't that a sham? Isn't that a fraud?

MARTIN LINSKY: Hodding, going back to the beginning, I understood you to say that television has no real substantive impact on the shaping of United States policy.

CARTER: That's right. And what's more, I promise you that the elite press, the establishment figures, the handful of those who comment in various areas with some substance, are far more important.

I was trying to say two things, and they are important because they are locked into a dance in which they have fine appreciation for the footwork of the other.

EUGENE PATTERSON: Should the press be forming policy?

CARTER: No. The presumptive duty of the government is to govern. The presumptive duty of the press is to print the facts. The press has no business in this area.

FANNING: What about when the camera zeroes in on a poor, starving family or on individuals who suddenly become news figures? Doesn't that influence policy in that it gets the public all stirred up?

CARTER: That suggests that 10.8 percent unemployment doesn't affect the administration, and only the picture of one unemployed worker out there will.

FANNING: But it has an emotional impact. If you were a Reagan administration supporter, you would be saying, well, our policies haven't had a chance to work yet and here is the press out there fomenting this revolution because of the glamorization of the poor unemployed workers. But it does have a focusing effect that does influence policy. I just can't believe it doesn't.

CARTER: I think the old argument always is why don't you show a picture of the 91.2 percent of the folks that are working and why do you do these little feature stories, sob stories?

FANNING: But it does have an impact.

CARTER: Of course it has an impact. But that impact doesn't have a life of its own.

LINSKY: Hodding, you don't feel it would be any different if they showed a picture of that child or put up a chart of unemployment?

CARTER: Of course it does.

LINSKY: And wouldn't it be different if they had a chart or if they had two talking-head economists putting unemployment in the context of everything else that's happening in the country?

CARTER: All of that's true.

LINSKY: They would all have different impacts on government, wouldn't they?

CARTER: They would have different impacts on the public perception of that evening's news.

LINSKY: And what the politicians do and what the people in Congress would say and the time frame in which you have to make a decision and who you've got to involve in the decision and how long you think you have before you have to get unemployment down?

CARTER: All of those things undoubtedly have their effect. But the congressman who comes back from Orange County, California, is going to have a different kind of audience response than the guy who comes back from Gary, Indiana, where that picture has some resonance in his own experience.

LINSKY: We're not talking about turning things upside down. But if you think you need a year to turn unemployment around, wouldn't you rather have a series of stories in the *New York Times* than those pictures on television every night?

CARTER: Yes. All I'm saying is, those were not a matter of concern to the administration in any case until such time as the reality was so bad that every reminder of it became an added elbow in the ribs.

64

FANNING: I really think that one of our biggest problems is that we are too sensitive and too quick to reach for the cloak of the First Amendment. We throw that cloak around our shoulders, we don't examine ourselves, we don't examine one another. We are the most thin-skinned element in this society. If the people we cover were as sensitive as we are about the few times we get the spotlight swung on us, we'd be in fistfights practically every day. We are just not self-examining enough and we are far too self-righteous.

LINSKY: Are things different in Great Britain? I mean, is there more self- criticism within the press?

HAROLD EVANS: There is a weekly program, which used to be on prime time with me on it, which is called "What the Papers Say." It examines the conduct of the national daily press every week. And it was very, very effective, with three or four different commentators. It was then scheduled for lousy time and it's now come back on prime time.

Television is monitoring the press in Britain in a way in which the press is not monitoring television.

CAPLAN: I wanted to ask a question about what the role of the media should be.

Should the exclusive aim of journalism—be it print or television—be the truth and the reporting of facts? Why does everyone seem to be leaning in the direction now that it is not the job of the media—ever—to set agendas? If we ask the question, should the media ever pursue justice in some way or another, then we can move on to the next question. Never set an agenda, in any area? Not even on the editorial page?

HOGE: I didn't mean that. I think one of the main functions of the press is defining the unfinished agenda of society. It doesn't necessarily mean that politicians will pick it up the next day.

The same is true of the constant rein that the press can put on issues or things which are being unaddressed. I've always felt that the great impact of an editorial page is not what it says on any particular day, but its force and credibility and character over a span of time. In that sense I think we have a very important role to play in society's job of setting agendas.

CAPLAN: So you might say not only is there a need to pursue justice, but there is a need to pursue justice for certain groups that might be left out, left aside.

HOGE: Yes indeed.

CAPLAN: A special focus there.

HOGE: Yes, I would say that.

CAPLAN: Well, if that's true, then what Hodding says about the inability to set agendas is true. There is a serious gap.

CARTER: Let me reenforce what Jim (Hoge) said, because to me the editorial page is the recurring effort to say whatever your fundamental beliefs are—not because you think you'll win tomorrow's victory, but because you're about the business of trying to influence the long term agenda and decisions that are to be made.

CAPLAN: I think that that's a good note to end on, and it's an interesting thing to think about, whether in fact that is the philosophy guiding editorial pages. Or is it not more the influence of TV—the temptation to jump on the TV bandwagon, forgetting that the real push should be to drive home these central issues—health care, science policy, what's going on with the infrastructure of the cities.

Have the Sailors Taken Over the Ship?

OPENING STATEMENTS BY:

Gaye Tuchman
James Batten
Roy Peter Clark

LOUIS HODGES: As you know, the subject of the morning is the role of reporters, whether or not the sailors have taken over the ship or the monkeys are running the zoo. We have as our initial leadership Gaye Tuchman, Jim Batten and Roy Peter Clark.

GAYE TUCHMAN: Having looked at the question, which asks have the sailors taken over the ship—I just wonder, how could they? The only way that sailors get to take over a ship is when the captain has done something egregious or has not done his job.

Actually, we could try to differentiate a little about what reporters can get away with, what kinds of things, and that might be what's meant by "taking over the ship."

In that sense, it's clear that newspaper reporters and writers have some ability to get away with things. That's not true for television reporters.

It's harder to edit a tape than it is to edit words—which means that a television reporter can indeed have more attachment to his words, and it also means that in some peculiar ways the people who deal with the television reporter can control him.

I really have a lot of trouble thinking about how reporters can take over the ship because it's clear that news is something that happens in some locations, and not in other locations, and can happen at some times of the day and not at other times of the day.

The work of reporting and of editing is organized as much as possible around the various power centers everybody has recognized. Reporters may get sent to stories about things that other people haven't seen before. But even if we're talking about whether they find things that other people haven't seen before, they're still finding them to put them in to some kind of frame, to put them in some kind of story form, and I don't mean a beginning, a middle and an end—but a "story form."

In the 1960s, for example, many social movements were covered like crime stories. It's not a crime to have political beliefs, and that becomes very pertinent in terms of the questions that were being asked yesterday about what it is the news media do.

I enjoyed the discovery of the scandal after Watergate. And it was nice to see Koreagate, or any other "gate" that anybody could think of. The same thing happened after the Teapot Dome scandal when all of a sudden a lot of people were discovering scandals all over the place because the stories could get into the newspaper.

So one begins to talk about what it is that the reporters do when they find something, and we're also talking about what it is that editors encourage them to see.

Things like the Janet Cooke story are a product of the same system that encourages scientists to fudge their data because of competitive pressures. Janet Cooke did a masterly job, after all, of finding a social problem in the city in which she lived, and which everybody cared about. Then she managed to turn it into a kind of event where it concerned a specific personality. It just happened that it turned out not to be true. But in every other sense it was a very good piece of reporting. That's why it got a prize. It wasn't an accident that somebody recognized the components that would make a story deserve that prize.

I want to just say two more things. One of them has to do with what it is that can or cannot be a fact, that Janet Cooke appeared to have gotten correctly. Maybe she understood what a fact was supposed to be. All of us must realize rules about sources and what it is that can be a fact.

A sociologist was giving a dissertation in California, hanging around with some reporters, when a bus came in to this small town with a dead bum aboard. As he watched, the bus driver went through the pockets of this dead bum and pulled out a Social Security card for a John Doe or some such name, and the reporter said to himself, "Aha, here we have a stiff carrying a Social Security card with the name of John Doe on it." Then a cop came, looked at the Social Security card and said, "Aha, John Doe died." At that point, John Doe was dead, because a cop had said it, using the exact evidence available to the reporter.

Now, of course, it came from a more official and appropriate source. That definition of fact and official sources is basic to the very way the news is covered, in the United States, at least. The centralized institutions in our society—usually big business or official institutions —determine what it is that's acceptable information for the rest of us.

JIM BATTEN: I want to go with a sprinkling of anecdotes and then a sprinkling of quotes from editors that I have asked the question of and then try to draw some conclusions from that. The first anecdotes involve the last paper I had, the *Charlotte Observer.*

The *Observer* is a paper that, as a lot of you know, has had a long and enormously honorable tradition of being on the enlightened side of the racial issue, particularly in years when that was not an easy thing to do. That kind of tradition, by 10 years ago, had attracted a staff of the kind that would be familiar to a lot of you: bright, able, idealistic, liberal, attracted to the *Observer* for the kind of paper it was on that issue and some others. They tended not to be from Charlotte, they tended not to be from North Carolina. Most of them weren't married, and the ones who were married didn't have any kids in the public schools. They didn't have any particularly strong indentification with the community.

Then, in the late sixties and early seventies and into the mid-seventies, you will remember that there was a tumultuous community debate, a trauma over busing, the landmark busing decisions and executions involved in Charlotte and Mecklenberg County.

The staff, I finally concluded, had a lot of trouble covering that story down the middle for reasons implicit in what I just said. I want to cite two specific examples of that.

One time we sent the education reporter to Alberta to interview the newly appointed school superintendant who was on his way to Charlotte, and I remember being astonished as I read his story on Saturday afternoon to find nothing in it about the new guy's opinion on busing and school desegregation.

I asked the reporter, how come? And he said, "Well he shouldn't have to deal with it, it's time for this community to put that issue behind it."

Another example is this. At one point we began to hear rumors that because kids were scared to go to the bathroom in their schools, some urologists in Charlotte were treating kids for problems that resulted from not going to the bathroom until they went home.

I couldn't tell whether that was a real story or whether that was just a wild rumor, but it obviously was worth trying to find an answer. I remember having a terribly difficult time interesting anybody in the story.

Bob Ingle, former managing editor of the *Miami Herald*, said this: "Both editors and reporters are too often uninterested in the stories that demonstrate government's efficiency and innovation. I recall once at the *Miami Herald* trying for weeks to persuade the city desk to do a story on the county manager's productivity team, an innovative approach that had saved taxpayers millions by streamlining operations of government. I virtually had to order the story done, because both the reporters and the editors could not see a valid story for fear of doing a puff piece on their historic adversary."

Another example. I won't use the name because this is secondhand, although I'm sure this is true, and some of you may have been in on the conversation. An editor whom we all know was confiding to friends in the last two or three weeks that he was enormously angry with himself, frustrated, because he had happened to attend a high school band competition in his city and had been much taken with it. He thought it deserved coverage in his newspaper. So he went back, and after talking to a number of people and suggesting in a number of ways that there should be a story, nothing appeared and apparently to this day still has not.

Now let me switch to four quotes that I think get at different aspects of what we're talking about:

"Some reporters feel driven to expose graft and corruption, even when none is proven to be there. Some editors give in, not so much because they're weak people, but because they want to be thought of as a part of this noble effort. They don't want to be linked with that questionable echelon of management that starts somewhere around the managing editor level.

"The folks who hobnob with local politicians and chamber of commerce types must share some of that taint."

Another one. "When we, and I suspect when other newspapers, launch an ambitious project, those undertakings often take on a life of their own. We put months in an investigation of zoning violations and there's a reluctance at the end to ask ourselves whether we really have the story we set out to do. Our commitment creates an anticipation which grows to a near demand that the stories be given the best possible play, even if they don't measure up."

Another one from a smaller paper. "In my role as a new editor, allowing reporters to do things that I was uneasy about, having had a liberal education and being exposed to tolerating the ideas of others, I often failed to put my foot down firmly enough. However, now that I've been burned a few dozen times, I have learned that it is indeed the editor's job to set the highest standards he knows, which means overruling reporters frequently."

One last quote. "It takes a hell of a lot more courage sometimes to make a decision that's unpopular with your staff than it takes to rake a public official over the coals. All of us believe that great newspapers are built by an editor with vision who recruits the most talented group of people available, and then lets them participate up and down the line of the decision making process.

"But it may well be that some editors have let democracy in the newsroom get out of hand. When we are hiring editors, we need to make sure that they understand that no editor who was unwilling to make unpopular decisions was ever a distinguished one."

I personally agree with all the points just made in the reports of different people. Why do we face that kind of problem? I want to emphasize that in my opinion, certainly whoever's fault it is, it is certainly not the reporter's fault.

The editor's job is to edit and to have a coherent vision of what his or her newspaper ought to be, and then effectively shepherding things in that direction. Too many editors abdicate that responsibility.

Why do they do that? Well, I think there are a bunch of reasons. One is that a lot of editors are too eager to be loved by their staffs, and they confuse morale, high morale, with real leadership.

Another aspect I think is that editors don't want to seem timid. Our system necessarily enshrines the virtues of aggressiveness, overcoming obstacles, getting the story, telling the story. Compassion is not one of our big values. And so it's pretty tough. Reporters or desk editors are raring to go with a story that may be wrong, but the editor really doesn't want to seem like a patsy.

Related to that I think is that editors don't want to seem to interfere with the normal functioning of the news gathering process, lest they be seen as favoring special interests, particularly perceived as establishmentarian interests.

I think that a lot of this kind of thing represents overreaction to the bad old days in our business when the advertising department would lobby and sometimes succeed in getting stories killed or getting stories on page one or getting stories in the paper at all. When coverage was cozy and uncritical and puffy, the editor's main goal in life was to keep his job and not let his paper offend anyone.

I think, coming from a slightly different angle, that if the sailors do take over the ship, there are all kinds of dangers, and not just to the issues of balance and fairness, but also to the priorities of coverage. The things that reporters want to write about are not necessarily the things that readers want to read about.

I've got one editor friend who says reporters in some ways have an inherent conflict of interest because they want to do things that are exciting, glamorous, prize winning and all that, and the readers may want to know who the new eighth grade teacher is.

I think even though we have made a lot of headway in the last 10 years, too many papers are still run to some degree more for their staffs than their readers.

I think the answer to all of this is not a return to the authoritarian, from the top down kind of thing. Everything these days hinges on productivity, work quality and pride in work. Workers do vastly better if they not only feel, but if they are genuinely involved in the decision making process. That is especially true for reporters who are their paper's eyes and ears, are sensing trends and seeing new things going on.

Papers that ignore their reporters' perceptions are not going to have good reporters for very long, and they won't deserve to.

I think finally what's called for is editorial leadership in the best sense, leadership that listens carefully to the staff open-mindedly and discerningly.

Finally, it is leadership that defines the vision and doesn't simply impose it but persuades the people who work for him that that is a worthy, legitimate vision for the 1980s.

ROY PETER CLARK: Before we can answer the question, have the sailors taken over the ship, we probably have to know which ship and perhaps which navy we're talking about.

In five years of playing confessor to hundreds of reporters and editors from most of your newspapers, I have come to the conclusion that there are at least two types of ships sailing the sea of journalism, perhaps three. For convenience, I will call them the *Nina*, the *Pinta* and the *Santa Maria*.

On the *Nina*, the sailors indeed run the ship. They have no choice, because on this ship there are no officers. "At my paper," said a young reporter to me, "there is no editing at all. Whatever I write goes in the paper. No one checks it for accuracy, libel, pornography or blasphemy." I'm not sure what the editors of this paper are doing. My guess is that they are involved in "administrative" tasks, keeping budgets, making out schedules, swatting flies in the computer system, and attending meetings, lots of meetings.

The editors have not always abdicated their responsibilities, it has been taken away from them. In such an atmosphere, it is easy for the writers to lose all sense that control and criticism and guidance are essential for responsibility and excellence in their work.

There is a legend that when one editor changed one word in one lead of a Dudley Clendinen *St. Petersburg Times* story, that Dudley padded in his stocking feet to the desk, arms akimbo, and pronounced, "We are not amused!"

At the *Boston Globe,* I am told, certain writers resist editing by threatening "to go to New York."

MICHAEL O'NEILL: Wow, what a threat!

CLARK: It is sad, but not surprising, to hear reporters refer to editors, as the "butchers," for it's true in many cases that editors themselves are badly equipped to handle the copy of headstrong and talented writers.

Perhaps the writers had been trained to seek new approaches to reporting the news, but work for editors who know only the old ways. An editor confronts a story written in a narrative, rather than a telegraph style, he's not sure what to do with it, so he makes the mistake of leaving it alone.

"My editors get mad at me," said one talented feature writer from Kansas. "They think I expect them to walk on water, and I do!"

"Reporters these days," says an editor from St. Louis, "expect their editors to have the long view and the short view, to be able to devote lots of time to their work, to be teachers and diagnosticians. Who could live up to that?"

"I'm afraid there is no one at this paper who could teach me anything," said one sports writer to me last spring. I've read his stories, and I can tell you that he is wrong!

Now we turn to the *Pinta,* and not to be confused with the *Pinto,* a ship that explodes from rear end collisions! The *Pinta* is a newspaper of the editors, by the editors and for the editors. At such a paper, the editors have special names for reporters. Writing coach Don Murray once heard editors at a newspaper referring to the writers as "the troops", and in certain moments, "those cocky pricks!" which if nothing else, is a world class tautology.

At such a paper, reporters never have any ideas, they only have assignments. The assignments come from above, from editors and publishers, from the friends of editors and publishers. They come from editors' meetings. Here's what one reporter told me recently: "They spend all their time at those goddam meetings. When they come out of those meetings, we know we're in for it. They think we're nothing more than conduits for their stupid ideas."

A ship where the officers have lots of meetings seems generally rigid in its interpretation of the news, and of the truth. Officers don't like surprises. A reporter was sent to south Boston to do a story on the outrage of its Irish inhabitants to the death of IRA hunger striker Bobby Sands.

Room was left on the front page for the story. The reporter went to the churches, the shops and saloons, and came back with the news that there was little reaction to the death of Bobby Sands. These people were worried about jobs, about schools. Moreover, they thought suicide was a mortal sin.

When the story did not meet the editor's preconceived notion, it was moved inside with the obits.

Reporters of such newspapers, in the words of one writer, are like "hired guns"—have pen will travel. One reporter described how he felt like a Rastafarian sandwich maker in the delis in New York. "What you want today, boss? You want cheese, I give you cheese. You want lettuce, I give you lettuce."

There is little vitality at such papers because ideas are imposed on the writers. The editor says it's time to do a piece on the mayor. Sometimes the assignment comes to the reporter with strings, or a chain letter of an editor's memo attached. The word for this practice at the *St. Petersburg Times,* I learned, was "poopie dust." I was told to always beware of stories with poopie dust on them.

Journalists can be trained to be devoid of all ideas. When Steve Lovelady arrived at the *Philadelphia Inquirer,* he was given a dozen reporters to work with. "I told them," said Steve, "that in the next six months, I wanted them to develop their own story ideas. They looked at me as if I was crazy, or speaking in another language. The concept was totally foreign to them."

A friend of an editor in New York took a ride on the Staten Island ferry and decided that it was filthy. Three memos came to the writer about the problem with a note: "Good idea." "Good idea." "Good idea." stamped to each one. The reporter rode the ferry. "The only thing I can truthfully write," he told his editor, "is that the Staten Island ferry is the cleanest form of mass transit in New York City!"

The editors couldn't believe it. The ferry must be filthy. The memos said so!

Clearly, most of the discretion at any newspaper is necessarily with reporters. They are the closest to the events we cover. As editors, you rarely know what facts were left in the reporter's notebook or which ones never reached his notebook at all.

I am prepared to argue that at a good newspaper, a good many ideas will percolate up from the reporters, rather than be imposed by the editors.

Finding the idea, I would argue, is the central act of writing well. That does not mean that the officers are giving up the ship, or that teamwork is impossible. It does not mean, if I may change the metaphor, that Lynn Swann can't use all of his moves because someone else is calling the plays.

The code words for responsibility at a newspaper are "collaboration, flexibility, communication and the inheritance of values." This is what happens on the *Santa Maria.*

This is the best sort of ship to sail on—destined to reach the New World. And for the purposes of our discussion, I have more questions than answers about how this ship works.

Is it possible to create an environment at a newspaper in which good work and ethical behavior are recognized and rewarded? What can we do to mend the central relationship of responsible journalism, that of writer and editor? Can we hire and train editors to do the job properly? Do we dare spend enough money to give them the time to be editors, to work with writers and to handle copy, to purify stories of inaccuracy and bias?

Is it possible to open lines of communication between reporters, editors, and two other important groups, those who read our stories and those who are the subjects of our investigations?

If an editor assigns a story, is he flexible enough to accept something that does not meet his preconceived notions as to how it should be written? Is the writer willing to change the focus or direction of a story based on advice from an editor? Do they talk enough to each other to make such things possible?

And finally, how does a newspaper pass down its most important values to its reporters and editors? Do the Top Dogs at the paper communicate these values through a memo or a homily or tantrum?

That may help, but it is not enough because if you will excuse the impertinence, you, top editors, do not work where the action is. Your managing editors, your city editors and department heads do.

In the words of David Hawpe, who is a managing editor in Louisville, the newsroom is their theater. By their looks, words and actions, they communicate what is important.

The values that are communicated are not always positive. Steve Lovelady was telling a story about another newspaper, not the *Philadelphia Inquirer,* where one assigning editor yelled at a new recruit for fraternizing with his peers. "Don't ever forget that those people are your enemies," she said, or reportedly said. "Your ability to survive here and to please me depends upon your ability to beat them." Would you like to sail on a ship run by sailors who consider each other as enemies?

An editor calls his best, most aggressive, most adversarial reporters "killers." If my friend Mike Foley calls you a killer, you've received his highest compliment.

Bob Greene, at a national convention of journalism teachers, referred to part of investigative reporting as "moving in on your target." One investigative reporter relishes the opportunity to go, "under cover". Language reflects attitudes, but also helps determine them.

I am tempted to argue that the prime indicator of newspaper value, the "NVI," is story play. What is most important to a paper is reflected in the way stories are played.

If I come to a newspaper, no one is likely to tell me in so many words, how I am doing. If they run my stories on page one, I have some idea. If they don't, my job as a reporter is to examine the page one stories, and find ways to write like that. If those stories are about government, I'm going to find a way to write about government. If they're about corruption in government...well, you've got the idea.

As a sidelight, I visited a newspaper that wanted to encourage writers to write shorter stories. I examined all the page one stories for a week, and they were all very long. I concluded that the editors were dumb.

Some newspapers are developing innovative ways to reward responsible work and to communicate the values of virtuous journalism. One such experiment is entitled, "How I Wrote The Story," and is being undertaken by the *Providence Journal-Bulletin.*

Each week or so, the editors select a story which they believe represents the best work of the paper. Then the reporter, or editor, is asked to write a narrative on the process of putting the story together. How were the important decisions made, what major problems were overcome, what doubts linger?

These are published for the whole staff; in a single document, new staffers can discern what is considered "quality work" and what are the working habits of the best practitioners.

We treasure in our culture those people who act according to their convictions against obvious self-interest.

Newspaper people have done that. I've read about Hodding Carter's dad. I've read about the other people who were writing editorials in the south during the civil rights era, who faced ridicule and ruin for the sake of civil rights.

I told you yesterday about the abuses during the death watch after the Air Florida Flight 90 crash.

I did not tell you about two *St. Petersburg Times* reporters—Tom French and Milo Geylin—who were there, and who called their editors that night during this event. They were having real problems with what was happening. They didn't want to harass these people.

Their editor—Michael Foley, to his credit—told them to be polite, low key and professional. They did not get the best quotes or the sexiest anecdotes in their story the next day. In one sense, they acted against their superficial interests in favor of higher ones, and it does not hurt to work for a newspaper that, on occasion, is capable of doing the same thing as an institution, in thinking of choosing a right over the bottom line.

I would argue simply that there are pockets of excellence and responsibility at every paper. More often than not, a newspaper is a mix of qualities from the *Nina*, and the *Pinta*. But alas, there are few ships like the *Santa Maria*. Good leadership can create collaboration, flexibility, communication, the inheritance of values to a newspaper.

What I am hearing from writers and editors tells me that such newspapers are rare. Call me negative, call me cynical, call me Ishmael.

B.J. PHILLIPS: When I read this topic, I really laughed at the idea of sailors taking over a ship, because newspapers are so poorly edited that it's a joke. Only someone who has moved from newspapers to writing in a situation where they really edit, as I have done, really knows how poorly edited your newspapers are.

I don't just mean the substitution of one adjective for another. I mean those structural things that have to do with organizing a story, thinking it through, making sure that if the reporter didn't know enough about George Wallace, that something happened in the editing process to refilter that.

I submit as proof for my argument any newspaper in the country. Just pick it up and read it. It's amazing to me how much the people who actually handle copy and reporters do nothing other than shove paper further down the pipeline. I just insulted you now, and I hope I won't frighten you by saying that since you put in computers, there is less editing going on, in part because the whole story never sits out in front any more.

Go home and ask the desk editor when was the last time he moved paragraphs around. I'll bet you'd be shocked to discover that it hasn't occurred within the last six months, in part because now there are no stories. There is a psychological barrier there. The story is never real. It's just a series of electronic blips, and more and more editors are simply throwing the relay switches that shove those electronic blips down and out through the tubes and eventually into print.

Those machines have degraded an already desperate situation of non-editing.

MARTIN LINSKY: It seems to me the issue this morning is whether there is a set of values, ethical values, that are shared by the management of the news institution. And secondly, if there is such a set, is it the responsibility of that news organization or management to inculcate those values, professional values, in the employees?

I guess third is, is there a way to do that? I thought when Roy (Clark) was talking about a student in my media ethics course last year who actually may have even talked to some of the people in this room. He decided he would write a paper on whether, when people are hired on major newspapers, anybody asks them what they believe in and whether they believe, for instance, that it's okay to interview people in a disaster situation. He found in talking to a lot of the papers, that people thought that was a ridiculous thing to do. It would be very hard to do, even if you could do it. We're probably looking for a different kind of value, in fact.

People said to him, "I don't think that's the kind of reporter I want to hire because I want someone whose instincts are more aggressive than that." We began to develop a picture during these conversations of the kind of value profile newspapers have. The only exception was Knight-Ridder which does a kind of testing that we didn't find anywhere else. I'm wondering what some of the people around this table feel about that. Are there any shared values? Can you inculcate them, should you inculcate them? Can you identify the roots of them in the people that you hire when you hire them?

EUGENE PATTERSON: The answer is yes, and these are values that can't be written down. A lot of newspapers DO write them down. They say, "We're going to be fair, we're going to be balanced, we're going to be compassionate, we're going to be a great newspaper." Are you? The proof is in the pudding. So those values grow out of the kind of people you assemble. They learn these values not by anything you say to them, but by example.

When the city editor of the *St. Petersburg Times* told those two reporters on the disaster watch "Take it easy," that word spread after they came back. Then they learn. That's the way Foley wants it. They like that, they get their bearings.

Bob Haiman wrote an obit himself because there was a tough one a few months ago. A man named Angel Perez died here in St. Petersburg, and this is still a fairly small town. Angel Perez had been chairman of the board of Florida Power Corporation. One

of Bob's reporters had sent him to prison because he
was victimizing the customers of Florida Power, a
regulated monopoly, by taking kickbacks for oil sup-
plied to run his furnaces during the oil crisis. $193,000
he raked off, and we proved it on page one. He was
a close personal friend of Bob's and mine. But we sent
him to jail, and he died a few months ago. How are
you going to write that obit? Here's a man, once a
pillar of the community, back here in shame, and suddenly you've got to write an obit.

So Haiman said, "I'll do that." He didn't beat
round the bush about the man's record. He told of the
great things he'd done, told of the fact he had been
in prison. But he went to the trouble of calling up some
people to get comments for this obituary and he got
the ideal quote. Right after he said he had gone to
prison, this friend of his said, "You know, Angel didn't
make many mistakes like that, but it was typical of
him to take his medicine when he did."

Now that took the sting out of the obituary, and
the family thanked us. But the whole paper sees that.

Also this Methodist Town generality that one of
our reporters got in the paper. I, and everyone right
down the chain of command, landed with both feet,
not on that reporter but on his editor. The word spread
in the newsroom. That was out of bounds. This is the
way they want it. And that's how your set of values
is formed.

LINSKY: I think that's right, but I wonder
whether it goes far enough. I wonder why, for instance, in these four stories, or anecdotes, that you
didn't say whether they should be written down,
whether they should be the subject of a meeting,
whether once a week or once every two weeks, there
should be meeting of the staff to talk about that, knowing that it goes on in beer halls in a random kind of
way.

I wonder, for instance, whether when an employee
is hired, he might not be asked about some of those
incidents, about how he feels about them, what will
he do, whether he thinks that's consistent with good
journalism or inconsistent with good journalism.

What I'm wondering is, is there a way of taking what I consider to be good works and institutionalizing them, so you get the greatest benefit you can.

PATTERSON: I think throughout any employment interview, you feel out this fellow to see what he's made of, or this woman, and whether he reacts the way that you want a *Times* reporter to react. It's just a part of the chemistry.

KATHERINE FANNING: In answer to what Martin was saying, I think you actually might detract by attempting to put these anecdotes on paper and make each of them extend to some sort of rules or lessons. I think that what Gene is talking about, the atmosphere of compassion and the atmosphere of concern for accuracy, is something that really can't be put on paper. It's something that is communicated in a better way in a newsroom than through written codes or written anecdotes or anything of that sort.

It's a feeling that the newspaper has. Maybe it can be done easier in a smaller newspaper than it can in a large one, but I would opt against anything written.

ARTHUR CAPLAN: I think, to be fair, the burden is on the philosophers, the social scientists, the academics. We haven't talked about it much but those who are trying to serve in a sense as outside commentators do, in fact, do the systemization.

When I said that I thought the burden of proof lay on the person who wants the exemption from ordinary moral principles, I meant that that's a general guideline, a norm that can be taught to somebody. You could say, "Look, we assume prima facie (that's what they like to say in philosophy) that there are some self-evident duties that we have as a moral person, and if you want to override those, it's up to you to prove and justify why that is in every case. But you do need to be ready to give your reasons."

That, of course, presumes that we know what the set of prima facie duties are, and those have to be systematized and set. Someone has a basic right to privacy, a certain amount of confidentiality. There is something that we recognize as truthfulness that has to be honored, and I think that can be systematized.

I don't think it has been done. I think the academic community and the philosophers, the theologians and whatever have the sense that we can do it, I'm not sure it has been done yet. Something is out there in terms of getting that table of values down. I think it could be done, although I don't necessarily believe it's the journalist's job to do the systematizing. There's a basic core of values that it is not permissible to override. People have basic rights that should not be infringed. When somebody says you're being too adversarial, you're kicking in my door when somebody dies, you're performing a sting operation in order to get the truth, you're somehow twisting the norms that ought to prevail about promise keeping and truthfulness. It's those things, that basic core of things, that we in philosophy think of as basic rights. These are being overridden, waived, stepped on. I think that's what people object to.

It's not so much the hostility factor, it's this idea that you can do anything in the name of or in the service of your goal, Mr. Professional, be it a doctor, a lawyer, or businessman. If you're a doctor you won't tell me if I have terminal cancer because you're afraid you're going to cause a tizzy in my family. We know what's best for you. We're not going to do something that ordinary morality demands, which is truthfulness between doctor and patient.

The public says be damned. You can't put your judgment, your judgment of an assessment of what the consequences are, above your right to know. And if you're going to override that one, you'd better have a better reason than simply saying it's going to be too tough for me to bear.

Where are the philosophers and the theologians to tell us what is that basic set of values that if we're going to override we'd better have good reasons for overriding? I don't think that list has been made, and I think it could be.

JAMES HOGE: I just wanted to shift for a moment back to another aspect of this problem. If we talk about disasters for a moment, or acts of terrorism, it seems to me we've got another lesson to learn.

A few years back there was a terrorist incident in Washington, and about the same time we had a terrorist incident in Chicago. We had some of the problems in coverage that newsmen had in Washington. So we convened a conference in Chicago called "Media and Terrorism," and we talked about pooling and some of the problems. One of the things that became very clear is that in incidents like that you can't have very effective pooling unless some mechanisms have been set up in advance.

Secondly, it breaks down very quickly if the information process and procedures with, say, the police are inadequate or inept.

One of the lessons that we brought out of that was that if we want to cooperate we've got to start when there is no terrorist incident shaping up. We also have to talk with the police on a periodic basis about information policies.

Another thing we learned was that when an incident breaks out the very top people in every organization have to get together and say this is what I intend to do, and here's my phone number day and night. What's yours?

HAROLD EVANS: I find what Mr. Caplan had to say fascinating and let me give you one particular ethical problem I had as editor. You may have a different response to that.

There was an Englishman in Rhodesia, when Ian Smith had taken over the country in an illegal occupation and sanctions had been imposed by the United Nations and the rest of the world to freeze Rhodesia out and bring it to heel. As you know, the sanctions didn't work.

Nonetheless, this Englishman smuggled out to me, through his wife, a lot of documents describing how the Germans and the Americans were helping to break the sanctions through banks, and it was a great story. He said he was sending me this material to hold in case anything happened to him.

Well, he was then arrested in Rhodesia for smuggling out currency, and was put in prison for four years. I had all the documents about the sanction breaking in my office, when the attorney general of the illegal Smith regime came to my office and said, "Don't publish that stuff. If you don't publish it, we'll let him out after 12 months. If you do publish it, we'll double his sentence."

What happened in this case was that one of my reporters had been in touch with the wife of this man called MacIntosh, and I knew nothing about this till the reporter came in and said, "Mrs. MacIntosh gave me some documents which her husband said might be useful if he got into difficulty."

So first of all, there was a question of the understanding of the reporter and the wife's understanding with her husband. That was one of the ethical problems.

It was very difficult to decide. First of all, I didn't think that the bargain between the wife and the reporter was explicit. It was vague.

Secondly was the question, which was more important, how would exposing sanctions-breaking by Rhodesia affect the lives of the blacks and the people held illegally there?

Thirdly, there was the freedom of this man. Could we take the word of the attorney general of Rhodesia that if we didn't print the stuff and gave him the copy back he would in fact honor his promise and release the man?

We took a long time to debate the question. In the end, I decided to run the whole stuff and to tell the story of the secret mission by the attorney general, on the argument that it was my duty to reveal what I could about the illegal sanctions-breaking. Secondly, I had not been party to any agreement, and perhaps the reporter hadn't been. And thirdly, there was the possibility that this man would have his sentence prolonged. In fact his sentence was increased. He was sentenced to a further two years and was in prison for four years altogether.

Now I don't know whether my colleagues would have done anything different. Some of you would, probably.

CAPLAN: It seems to me that the relevant principle here was the question of could reporters accept information with conditions and strings attached.

In this case, the guy was trying to use the paper as an insurance mechanism for his safety. It's not clear what went on between the reporter and the man, in terms of what was promised, agreed to, negotiated.

If there really was a promise, I think it should have been honored. I don't like the notion that the editor wasn't a party to the bargain, that the editor somehow escapes the obligation to honor the promise because he didn't happen to be in the room.

It seems to me when the reporter is negotiating he is negotiating for the paper. That troubles me.

I think editors, in a sense, are indirectly bindable by the promise-making of their reporters, and if they don't want that, then they'd better be sure that they're aggressively pursuing what their reporters do, and vice versa.

The ambiguity of this promise leads me to think, however, it was truly not clear exactly what the circumstances were for the arrival of the information; that even though this man's interests would have been sacrificed, the longer term interests of releasing information that would affect many justifies the behavior.

I'd like to go back and interview the reporter and find out if he promised to meet the man's conditions and take the information under those circumstances? Then I would say, no, it wasn't right to go off the hook by saying, "Well, I'm the editor, I'm the publisher, I'm another reporter, I didn't promise. Let me see those papers. I'll run 'em. You know, I made no promise."

That's not right. When one makes a promise with the public or a source, one is promising as an institution, not as an individual.

HODDING CARTER: Can I ask a question? I know just from my show that there are at least some papers left in this country where you don't have to worry about reporter power or the sailors running a ship, where papers are ordered to see to it that a certain guy gets to be chief of police, like in St. Louis, where papers are ordered to pursue a certain course because it's going to help in a deal for an airline franchise.

Now let me ask a second question. I can give you nine out of ten newspapers in Mississippi in which a reporter had never heard of reporter power. Is it, in fact, what is defined as news, and does it really determine whether there is any power there at all?

These reporters are not allowed to cover anything which in any way presents any kind of problems for the established order in the community, and this is beyond race. We're not talking now about race, I'm just talking about what they're allowed to cover.

I ask you again, how many newspapers are there which are run in the don't-shake-up-anything-out-there, or if you're going to shake it up, shake up what I tell you to shake up. And how many of them are run in ways in which they, in fact, have the initiating power as reporters.

CLARK: One answer to that, or another element of the equation, is how much the newspaper is willing to commit in terms of money and resources, numbers of reporters, numbers of editors, the editorial staff. Sometimes it's not a matter of saying you cannot shake up the established order. When you've got one reporter doing the job of three, that person is chained to a desk, gets a lot of stories by telephone, and is incapable in most cases of doing stories which have significant impact. There are a lot of papers like that.

Reporters come to me saying, "I would love to do the sort of things that you're talking about, but here is how I work." They work on small staffs with limited resources.

TUCHMAN: I think that if you're talking about the question that Gene (Patterson) raised about how things filter down, an awful lot of what filters down in most papers is, if you do this story this particular way that upsets particular people, your editor is going to exclude it.

I'm not talking about big city papers or the "good" papers, I'm talking about most papers.

I suspect that what does filter down to the reporter, and what sets the tone in most newsrooms is not only the kind of overwork that Roy is talking about, but that if you try to see something in a really fresh way, critical of the institutions or the people in your city, you're going to be told to rewrite it. Actually you don't need to be told.

You don't need to be told to rewrite it every day. You just need one person to be told to rewrite it every couple of years and that story remains in circulation. People who work on that particular newspaper know that their freedom is limited. Just as Gene can give you examples of doing the right thing once or twice, and it gets around, the same thing goes in the other direction. That's the way I think it mostly works.

CARTER: Let me give you a larger perspective. I'm doing initial research on American correspondents in the Soviet Union. I've talked to about 25 former reporters who worked there and have come out, and I'm getting ready to talk to the ones who are working there now.

The average reporter says I learned very quickly that what my paper wanted was stories about dissidents, military operations and confrontations. Every time I tried to do a story giving some feeling of the flavor of the Soviet Union it was killed or it wasn't run. So I got a very quick message: What we want you to do is do the death watch on Brezhnev and we want you to do to dissidents and we want you to do confrontations.

TUCHMAN: Can I cite something that's even more peculiar? I have a friend who has been interviewing two groups of reporters, reporters coming back from the Soviet Union and the Soviet reporters in New York. And the match of how it is that they do their job is fantastically close, in terms of what kind of sources they go to, the kind of limitations there are on their activities, which kind of media they use and what kind of stories they're supposed to emphasize. It's shocking.

BOB HAIMAN: Most reporters do regard themselves as having a prime obligation to guarantee that the newspaper is operated with honesty and integrity, that their publisher's friends don't get off the hook or beyond the hook, and the extent to which that flame burns I think is positively correlated with the way they perceive the paper being run.

If they work for Mike Gartner they know that he's a tough minded editor and he takes no nonsense from the establishment in Des Moines, Iowa. Then they sort of turn the flame down a little bit because they know that its purity is safe at the highest levels.

But should Gartner leave and should a new editor with a different set of standards come in, a set of standards they perceive as lower standards, the flame never went out, and boy, can it be turned up on your Bunsen burner. Then they will say, "Well, you know, Gartner used to run this shop right, but this new guy, we'll have to provide the honesty, we will provide purity, we will make sure that those bastards don't get away with murder."

I resent their arrogance at times or their notion that somehow they are more honest than I am. But on the other hand, it's not completely discomforting. I don't think we should find it discomforting to know that out there in the city room are people who share these values that we say we hold, and if we ever wake up one morning with a blind eye, they're going to open that eye for us.

CLARK: I'm wondering if the group believes or accepts the trickle down notion of ethics at newspapers. I mean, is it enough to show good example, or do we need to have some organized ways of educating our staffs and ourselves that do not now exist perhaps in newspapers. Do we need to make newspapers more collegial in a way that we share ideas and values?

O'NEILL: I strongly subscribe to Jim Hoge's concept of creating a total atmosphere, mood, ethical context if you will, and out of that I think you're going to get a lot more results than trying to codify everything that humankind is trying to do.

I would also, however, underline the point that (Bill) Thomas made, and I think it's the greatest single problem I had or the biggest single failure that I was associated with, and that is communication. I think that you get so chewed up every day with this crisis or that, that you do not do enough talking back and forth with the staff. I think there should be a lot more of that, and that would help reinforce the kind of atmosphere that you're trying to create.

C.K. McCLATCHY: Going back to something Mike (O'Neill) said earlier, I think that the problem he described in having to decide that they were not going to run a particular story is an important example. The reverse is that you can't overstate what seems to be the importance among a lot of editors of being well thought of, of being popular. You can almost go into a newsroom and see how well run it is, and determine how this man is achieving his popularity. You're going to find that most really good editors are going to be popular anyway and run the room well. If he's not a good editor, sometimes he's going to be popular at the sacrifice of not making the sort of decision he might make.

It's much easier for an editor to tell a guy who comes in off the street to "shove off" than it is to say "no" to a group of reporters who come in and say, "We don't like this, we don't want you to do that."

A weak editor who is looking for popularity is always going to tip in the wrong direction in that situation. He will be popular with the reporters by saying, "Oh, gosh, you're right on, and we won't run that story (or we will run that story.)"

I don't know how you're going to get at this problem or what to do about it, but I've certainly seen it, and I guess the way you get at it is to have better editors who are willing to make the difficult decisions.

BATTEN: When I went back to Charlotte in 1972 one of the very trendy things I discovered going on was lots of police brutality stories, and there was a lot of basis for it at the time. But the stories were just miserably done, and no self-respecting editor ought to have been put in charge of that paper.

So I said, "When you figure out how to do police brutality stories, we'll start doing them again."

Well, the word went forth that Batten was soft on police brutality, and I really suffered for that for several months until they finally figured out how to do those kind of stories and did them right. Then I started putting them in the paper. Everybody felt a little better about police brutality.

CAPLAN: Bob (Haiman), I wanted to ask you something about playing to an image. I was thinking it might be that if you worked at a paper where you had an editor you trusted, you might turn the flame up, not because you felt you had to compensate for something, but because you knew that the editor was there as a governor. So you would work harder and maybe even go further or press harder because you were depending on the editor to cut you back. It's a way of dropping off some self regulation or trying to be your own editor because you trust the person who you're going to report things back to, to select and edit and make judgments.

HAIMAN: So what you're saying then is that it's harder to be a good editor than a weak one. And if you do encourage the staff to push, then that staff is going to push, and sometimes you will have to say, "Hey, you're pushing wrong on this one."

Summing Up

OPENING STATEMENTS BY:

Arthur Caplan
Harold Evans

LOUIS HODGES: The remainder of our time together is to be a general discussion of ethical problems, and our two speakers are Arthur Caplan and Harold Evans. I think that we'll do what we've done before. We'll hear from both of them before we argue with either of them.

So we'll now turn the matter over to you, Art, to give us your word.

ARTHUR CAPLAN: I was asked to talk about ethical problems facing newspapers—what can be done and what are the alternatives.

This is an interesting assignment for me, since I don't know much about journalism, and being a person trained in philosophy, I have never thought about practical alternatives.

However, I have tried to listen carefully and have decided that I could be most useful by reflecting upon some activities in a parallel profession that has been thinking and talking about moral issues. That is medicine, and for a living I watch ethical issues in science and medicine.

I have been involved in teaching at a medical school and working at the Hastings Center, dealing with medical organizations and medical schools. I try to introduce ethics and values concerns into the curriculum of those schools and into the medical profession and the scientific disciplines.

I think it might be interesting to describe for you some of the alternatives that have taken place in medicine so that at least you can compare and contrast and think about structural analogues that might be useful or not useful, hopeless or wonderful.

I did take as my general topic the kind of question that we started out with yesterday on the adversarial issue.

I've been listening to different people talk, and it seems to me that one issue we have shuffled aside occasionally is the question of whether a single morality can govern the behavior of all types and levels of personnel in the press, and whether a single set of moral guidelines can govern all press functions?

I tend to think that the answer to that will be, no—that editors, desk editors, reporters, and people in advertising will have different jobs to do, will have different functions to perform, and there won't necessarily be a single set of ethical beliefs, principles and values to guide their behavior.

So if you think we're going to find a single answer to what the ethics of the press should be, that seems to me to be the wrong way to be thinking.

We have tended to talk about things like fairness, compassion, thoroughness, and to say, "Well, those kind of things don't help much because they are not really rooted in the specific person's activities within a specific press context, whether it's television or radio or print media."

I think there are big differences between not only the jobs that people are doing, but where they are doing them. I think magazines are going to be different from newspapers and newspapers will be different from television, and different rules may apply.

So, one general assumption that I'd like to keep in mind is that when I talk about "alternatives" I will be talking generally about medicine. But in medicine, too, different people are doing different activities.

A lot of the things I'm talking about do not apply to the ordinary doctor in an office practice. The kinds of activities that I'm going to be remarking about and the structural changes that have taken place in medicine over the past 15 years pertaining to medical ethics concern medical institutions that are usually affiliated with medical schools. That's the particular community that I have had experience with and have talked to the most.

If you give an address to the state medical society or the county medical society and the doctors seem to care little about medical ethics, that may be true, — but that's not the data base I'm operating on.

What I'm talking about is, primarily, the elite of medicine, which might in some ways correspond to some of the institutions represented from journalism in this room. We have in medicine the *Washington Post* and the *New York Times* and the three networks.

There are the equivalents. There is the Harvard
Medical School, there is Stanford Medical School,
there is Columbia, there is Cornell. These are the
places that I've had more access to and the opportunity to talk with people there about what they're up to.

They're big tertiary care hospitals. They deal with
very sick people. They're in the business of treating
serious diseases. They are in the business of educating
students who will go on to highly specialized practices,
and most of them will tend to stay within the circuit
of elite institutions of medicine.

So that's the bias in my data sampling and my
experience. I'm not talking about nurses. I'm not talking about social workers. I'm not talking about GP's
and other people who are out in private practice, and
how medical ethics has affected their lives.

I said I was interested in the complaints about
adversarialness, and this seems to me to have been
bandied about in the room in different ways. People
have said, "Well, what does that really mean? Does
it mean that the press is too hostile, too mean, too
angry, not constructive enough?"

This same issue comes up in medicine. People complain that doctors are not sensitive enough to their
patients. And what happens when people in medicine
hear those complaints? Doctors say "Give me a case.
Who? Which doctor? Who are you talking about? Give
me an example!"

In fact, you can go through this same kind of
chasing-your-tail kind of exercise in medicine, but I
appeal to you on the grounds of familiarity to think
about it for yourself. All of us know that something
is a little bit wrong in medicine in terms of the kind
of care being delivered, in the kinds of care and concern that go on between doctor and patient. But people out there also know that something is not right
about journalism and they want some kind of change.

If you press people and say "Cite me an instance.
Give me a case. Who are you talking about?" They
can do it to some extent, but they can't do it very well.
This allows doctors to get off the hook.

What they say is you can't cite cases, so it's not true that people are unhappy. That flies against at least my sociological surveys, and it allows them to invoke a version of philosophy that I have heard for two days here—Bad Appleism! It's only the bad apples in the medical profession that bring the anger and invective of the public down on our heads. If we could clean them out —the drunks, the alcoholics, the boozers, the sexual philanderers—things would be better. Things are fine at National, things are pretty good at Mt. Sinai, things are fine at Sloane Kettering, it's just those creeps out in the boonies. They are driving us into the ground! All these sleazy operators are responsible for the bad reputation of our profession.

I think that Bad Appleism is a convenient moral out, but it is not an explanation of medicine, nor is it one in journalism, for this perceived discontent about how the profession operates.

I think, in fact, there has been some effort on the part of the medical profession to respond to complaints about inappropriate or poor performance by physicians in terms of their ethical conduct.

About 15 years ago medicine began to recognize, at least the elite institutions I'm talking about, that something should be done within medicine to change the conduct and behavior of professionals within that field. What made that profession shift? Let's see whether there are any parallels, forces, that might be applied or may not be applied within journalism.

One force in medicine developed as some leading figures in medicine came out in leading journals, naming people involved in immoral conduct.

I think the single most important force in changing medicine's mind about whether it had a problem in terms of the ethical conduct of its professionals and the way that people were relating to patients, and whether they ought to do something about it, was Harry Beecher, an anesthesiologist from Harvard, a distinguished figure in the field. In 1966 he wrote a lead article in the *New England Journal of Medicine,* called "Moral Problems in Medicine in Human

Experimentation" and he listed 15 cases of his colleagues, friends and peers. He named names and listed places and he said, "I'm presenting to you cases where I think the behavior is suspect, wrong, suspicious, bad and lousy".

The New England Journal ran it, and that is the most powerful organ of medical journalism around. Everybody reads it and no one could believe that Harry Beecher, this mild mannered, distinguished physician had actually gone on record and blown the whistle on the profession in its most powerful publication.

That probably was the single most important factor, sociologically speaking, in getting the profession to pay attention to the complaints, those general and disparate and vague and kind of unwashed moanings that were going on out there.

What am I talking about? I'm talking about Harry Beecher's article that described the Tuskeegee experiment in 1966. Harry Beecher's article released information on the Willowbrook experiments in which hepatitis infection was given deliberately to children in a state hospital, and the Brooklyn Chronic Disease Hospital case in which physicians injected patients with cancer to see what would happen.

Those were all presented. They were known about within the profession, they were talked about anecdotely, just as we sit around here and talk anecdotely about different crimes and what have you. But Beecher said, "I'm going public, I'm naming names."

A storm rippled right through the medical profession, as letters came in and people began to write articles defending the behavior. But that was, in fact, the profession's recognition that it had serious difficulties that had to be attended to. Remember, the business of the *New England Journal of Medicine* is not to report on the ethical conduct of its practitioners; it is to report clinical information and test information for use in changing medical practice. That leads me to point number two.

A key step in changing the profession's attitude was that it opened its doors to the legitimacy of talking about ethics. Ethics wasn't a beat for the *New England Journal of Medicine.* Nobody ever wrote about ethics there or in the *Journal of Clinical Investigation.*

If we went out to the library today and looked at the leading medical journals, of which there are roughly 20 that are read by most physicians or researchers, we would find in almost every issue one article devoted to ethics.

Franz Ingelfinger was the editor of the *New England Journal* and he created a beat called medical ethics.

He said that people could write articles about ethics and the *Journal* would run them. It was unheard of. If you think it's bizarre to think about the media reporting on its own ethics, or reporting on each other, imagine what it was like for a group of physicians, used to deferential behavior, to be told by journal editors that they were going to create in the leading publications a department called "medical ethics." Moreover, people were going to write on this subject and it would be published right next to reports on C Beta Cyanide 7 and its effect on cardiac function.

I don't know that there are any outside institutes, organizations or societies spending full time trying to track down ethical issues in journalism. But there are some in medicine. There are in fact a number of them. The medical profession willingly involved itself in certain forms of self-regulation. Systems like institutional review boards which now watchdog experimentation and professional society review organizations were set up in all states.

These groups are run by medical people to watchdog sensitive areas like human experimentation, but lay persons sit on all of these bodies. That seems to me to make a big difference, not only in terms of the input, but in terms of publicity. Doctors get a better public image because they invite laymen to sit on the regulatory panels.

HAROLD EVANS: It's been a fascinating session. And one of the echoes, one of the reverberations I have is that every foreign officer who has come to the United States, as a press officer or an academic, from de Tocqueville to Bryce, Dickens, Stevenson and Kipling, have all remarked about the tremendous theocratic strain in American journalism. American journalists have always seen themselves as kind of ink-stained Jehovahs.

A moral self-righteousness has always been the bane of the United States press. Charles Dickens tells the story of the anger of a journalist on a packet steamer when he wasn't given a complimentary crate of champagne, and the outrage this journalist vented upon the captain of the steamer.

There's no doubt about it. All these people were shocked at the ferocity of the American press, disguised as super-heated public virtue.

What's quite interesting about this is that until about 1900 in the United States, the term used to describe a good journalist was to say he had a vitriolic pen. It was a term of praise. And this was symptomatic of the range of journalistic messiahs and the will of heaven which tended to be the general ethical background of American journalism as perceived by foreigners.

I think now, however, the theocratic strain is greatly diminished in the United States. And I think it's still there. I mean, basically Mike O'Neill has taken a theocratic position. And if you read Ben Bradlee from the other side, it's quite significant that in his reference to relationships with the government, Bradlee talks about "the devil" in his letter.

That's something which rings strange to me. We're not in any kind of active conspiracy with governments in Europe. But the idea that the government is the devil is, I think, still a sediment of this theocratic strain which is exhibited by the Rev. Ben Bradlee and the counterattack from the other side.

I think that if Dickens came back today he would write a different story. And my impression of the American press is a kind of blandness. Of your 1,740 daily papers I would imagine 1,700 of them are pretty bland and are not very adversarial or very gritty.

As for the question that Mike raised, I think it's really a question of performance of the press, which is a wider issue than simply its relations with government and its relations with people.

I should tell you that this view of mine is supported by Jim Batten's reference to the Gallup Poll showing that only 42 percent of the people in a national sample said they had a great deal or quite a lot of confidence in newspapers.

A few years ago I did a study of this for the *Sunday Times* and commissioned a special opinion poll on the rating of the press people and what power they were thought to have.

In the United Kingdom, the figures came out like this: the most trusted were doctors, 75 percent with only 1 percent finding them the least trustworthy. Judges were 55 percent and least trusted 2 percent. Lawyers were 23 percent and civil servants 7. Four percent found members of parliament most trusted and 30 percent most distrusted. And ranking even below that were journalists with 4 percent finding them trustworthy and 34 percent untrustworthy.

More than one-third of the population found journalists untrustworthy. If, however, you take their power perception, the prime minister had 3 percent and 7 percent thought he had little sway. Newspapers and television: 23 percent thought that newspapers and television had the most sway, with 10 percent against. So newspapers and television are seen as having great sway but are fantastically distrusted.

There's a very good reason for this. The British press exhibits a degree of adversarialness and political bias which would keep Mike on his feet for the rest of the century.

It's not just the Murdoch press. You take the *Daily Telegraph,* the *Daily Express,* the *Daily Mail.* They perform a journalistic feat which is, I think, a litmus paper test of professional competence. They can take a source from the Labor Party—a Labor Party report and document—and write it up and present it as though it was a hostile story about the Labor Party. They can take a story about anybody of liberal inclination and present it with headlines which suggest the opposite of what the man said.

So the bias of distortion is not only rampant in the selection of news stories. The bias is right there in the news columns.

I think that our opinion poll figures compared with yours suggest that in fact you're in better shape than the British press in terms of bias. And one reason for this, I think, is that you've always taken seriously the question of press performance.

Some people in the profession have reacted hostilely to the valuable speech by Mike O'Neill because there's some very strange bedfellows who share the professional anxieties that you all share about a free and efficient press.

I'm alarmed when Kurt Luedtke, one of the writers on our reading list, asks whether we are more free than Britain, France and Scandinavia. Their press is less free—correct. Then he goes on to say they have elected to restrain. They never elected. Nobody ever asked them. Nobody ever asked them, do you want to restrict the press? The press in those countries has become restricted by an accretion of common law decisions, by statute, by inertia, by habit and lousy press behavior leading to restriction and leading to no support for freedom.

Then Luedtke goes on to say their citizens are every bit as free as we are. Well, it's just not true. Similarly, when Max Kampelman says that the British seem to get on all right despite the fact that their restrictions are great, that again is not true.

When you get some of the critics of the press making comparisons with Europe or Britain they say look, those guys don't have the freedoms that you in the United States do but they manage. The truth is, they don't manage.

For instance, if you want to find out whether it's safe to eat on a cruise liner, you can't find out in England.

We have to come to the United States, to Washington, and under the Freedom of Information Act we can get hold of the inspector's report on whether it's safe to eat on the *Queen Elizabeth* or whatever it is, then publish that. You cannot get that information in the United Kingdom.

Similarly, for instance, you have here a right to know whether dyes are used in foodstuffs. You're not allowed to know that in the United Kingdom. In Britain there's a dye called FK Dye which is used in kippers. Here you can find it out very easily. In Britain you can't.

That goes through a whole range of political, economic and social questions, from medicine to old age, to treatment in mental hospitals. So don't fall for any of this stuff that what the press needs is laws similar to those in England, because there we have some of the worst newspapers in the world.

Political bias in England is okay. You can be as biased as you like. You can trample all over people in gossip columns, which are very malicious. But when it comes to finding out facts in the public interest, you're restricted from doing so.

So the antidote to some of the problems we see in the United States doesn't in my judgment lie in greater legal restrictions, nor in encouraging those people who suggest that the comparison is all forced.

The curious thing is, and it's an interesting philosophical point, that the doctrines of free speech which were bequeathed to us by Milton and John Stuart Mill are all to do with freedom to make statements with the pen. Those classical philosophers assumed that there was a free flow of facts, like the classical economists assumed there was a free market in goods. In fact there isn't a free flow of facts. And much more importantly nowadays in England, and in some cases in this country, it's not the freedom to have the opinion but the freedom to have the facts on which an opinion can be based.

So that, it seems to me, has been the real battle. It's important that you continue to win because you're still the only laboratory in the world for what a free press can do. Everybody suffers when you have misdemeanors of the kind you do, because then it's used against us in England.

That's very devastating. The effect of printing grand jury leaks or in trying people in the headlines is, I think, extremely damaging in this country and devastating elsewhere because it seems that the experiment has gone off the rails.

Libel is extremely difficult in England, but it's nonetheless possible to do very good investigative journalism because it's good discipline for reporters to have to prove the truth.

I would not want to have edited a paper in Britain if we could have exposed wrongdoings by saying we reasonably believe this to be true. I think it would have been a luxury which we managed to do without.

In 15 years of editing the *Sunday Times* we lost not a single libel action because the reporters had the discipline to prove the facts which they were alleging about fraud or about malfeasance of one kind or another.

In terms of agenda-setting, I think the most important thing that the press can do in terms of agenda setting is to remember the primacy of original reporting.

One of the things which bothers me about some of the critics, including Kampelman, is that he talks of normal reporting when he really means event reporting. That's important. Some of the most important reporting is initiative reporting.

We identify issues, whether it be mental health care or prisons. And making those difficult subjects interesting seems to me to be one of the challenges of modern journalism.

One problem I've had with this whole session is that we keep talking about the press when we're really talking about the *New York Times,* the *Washington Post,* ABC, NBC, CBS and possibly the *Wall Street Journal.* The real problem in this country is that the leadership is confined to those areas of concern and anxieties which have been expressed elsewhere and not properly focused.

That, it seems to me, possibly was on Mike O'Neill's mind in speaking about that particular leadership.

HODDING CARTER: First, let me plead guilty to delivery of the statement on agenda setting. My point remains, however, that I've heard it said that the press sets a national agenda. I simply reject that.

Second, on the overall question of who monitors press performance, the *Los Angeles Times* and some other papers do a very good job. Roughly two dozen other papers have ombudsmen in their newsrooms, but there are few outsiders involved.

There are less than a half dozen news councils of any sort in this country and the National News Council seems to spend a great deal of time self-consciously not cooperating with almost all major organs of the press in the country.

Journalism is not a profession in this country which takes lightly the idea that there should be any kind of monitoring, except that expressed by the selection of letters to the editor which it deigns to print out of the thousands that come in.

B. J. PHILLIPS: I think it's obvious that the reason we're here is that we're worried about ourselves, and we'd like to arrange a pre-emptive strike so that regulation doesn't come and get us, either slowly or in a big sudden way, which can happen in a democracy because majority rule, or at least majority hysteria, can push something through.

So we'd like a pre-emptive strike. We're worried about our excesses and our abuses and our anguish and our behavior. I think that what we've been doing here for the past few days is trying to grope our way to knowing how we're supposed to act. What stars do we navigate by? Do we confront these ethical problems?

If we're groping for ways to act, maybe we ought to remember what it is in the end that jurors have to do. They look their neighbors in the eye and answer the question: Was this appropriate behavior?

JAMES HOGE: I hope I can say what I'm about to say without being misunderstood. I am troubled because I've heard for two days now what I consider to be a fairly general overstatement, both about how the public views us and the nature of our current sins and about the threats which are confronting us.

Let me take each one of these. I've looked at a lot of research, too, that says people hate us, they fear us, they want to punish us. I don't dispute it. But I think it has to be put in some larger context. It depends on what questions you ask.

I think even when people say that is the way they feel about us, and that is what they want to do to us, that upon reflection and when pushed to real action you'll find they have a much more complex view of the press. It may be quite grudging, and it may be with some aspects of disrespect, but they understand its utility in this society of ours.

I don't agree that we don't pick it up in our educative process. Let's just take one group, business leaders. We've all had this phenomenon of being beaten over the head by businessmen who tell us we don't know how to report economics, don't know how to report on their companies. We send ill-trained reporters to interview them. We send reporters with anti-business biases.

But almost invariably what it ends up with in such discussions is look, we are not saying we want legislation to tell you what you can do and what you can't do. We are just asking you to police yourselves. They believe in the First Amendment in a very pragmatic way almost as firmly as we do.

What I think I read much more, and which I think is an appropriate response these days, is that for good or ill reasons the public has decided that indeed the press in this country is a more powerful institution than it once was, and indeed, in some ways it may be too powerful.

Therefore, there is a kind of natural instinct to reject that power, to be a bit more skeptical. After all, that is what we expect of people in a democracy, which is that they remain skeptical—not disbelieving, but skeptical of all centers of power. I would say, for example, that if we look at the legal record during the last 10 or 15 years every time major cases have come up alarm bells go off and red flags are hoisted. If you take those decisions as a whole, however, they have been more favorable rather than less to the press. We have a freer press today.

I think the move on the libel front these days, some of the jury decisions, are an expression of the public's desire to check us as well as to punish us. They are moves to rectify what they think are probably too loose an environment for us.

Therefore, we may see some tightening up of libel laws. But I submit that there's a great deal of difference between this kind of incremental adjustment and a wholesale repeal of the First Amendment.

I've not sensed that that is on our horizon, that anybody wants that or that we have done things that would justify large parts of this society feeling that way.

I also think that over the past decade there has been a lot done in our business. We have some self-examination and have set up some critical mechanisms, reasserting editorial authority. It has us on a path that has left plenty for us to discuss in these last few days, but at least we are on a path and recognize some of the things we've got to deal with.

So as I said, I don't want to be misunderstood. There are some things we should be concerned about. But I think you misassess the public attitude toward us, the real legal and judicial track record that we're working with.

KATHERINE FANNING: I think it is the big press that has the problem—the networks, the news magazines, the *Washington Post* and *New York Times* that perhaps have been perceived as arrogant and insensitive to the concerns of the little man.

I think we should remember, however, that those organizations trickle down to us way out in the boondocks and on the frontier. We subscribe to those news services, the *L.A. Times-Washington Post,* the *New*

York Times. The reporting appears in our newspapers,and it is the role model for the profession.

So I think what is done by those major newspapers in a leadership position is terribly important. I liked the idea thrown out briefly yesterday as something to consider. It's to me a fairly new idea that in the case of extreme tragedy and sensitive situations we consider something like pooling—not inundating someone who has just lost a whole family in a tornado or something of that sort with 35 reporters, but perhaps letting them deal with one or two.

Obviously that poses all kinds of problems and dangers and it could never be codified or legislated, but there could be a consciousness of the dignity of the individual. I think that would go a long way toward improving our image, if that's the proper word.

It's a real concern to me that we like to peek so much into peoples' private feelings that often it goes way past any news value to savor others' tragedies.

This is one of my concerns. I think we could have an impact without in any way inhibiting public responsibility, the public's right to know. I question whether the public really has the right to know how deeply someone is hurt on the occasion of losing a family or whatever. And I think it's been valuable to discuss things of that nature here.

CARTER: If the reason we came here was because we feared that there was some gathering assault on the First Amendment or the power and independence of the press, we could have gone home yesterday. Whatever crest there was on that one has passed for the time being. And I would suggest to you that the reason for concern is precisely because as an institution the press gets more and more beyond the kinds of prescriptions which people want their institutions to have to be responsible to.

I would suggest to you the reason we're here is that we have at least some conscience about what it is that we're supposed to be doing with what in this sense is very real power.

Now, let me deal with two sides of this. I happen to agree that the average American paper is indeed so bland as to make me wonder whether it understands that there are greater issues out there. The problem with most papers that I see is that they don't seem to know, nor do they wish to be told, that there's a problem in River City.

That's the way most of them are, and you all know that. Those of you who go to your state press conventions know that, and there we are.

On the other side, however, while Jim (Hoge) says the trends are toward our being more responsible to these perceptions of the public's concerns with our power and with our mistakes, the fact is the trends are not. The trends are simply not trending at all. There are fewer press councils than there were a few years ago. There are no more ombudsmen than there have ever been. There are no indications that in some organized, systematic way the public can see that there are any avenues for the public at large to have its feelings of unhappiness receive a hearing. They just don't exist.

JAMES BATTEN: In every community every year there are issues that newsrooms have the unwitting capacity to be unfair or unbalanced about.

It seems to me that every editor, as a conscious exercise, ought to decide in his own head what that list is in his town. Then he should be particularly watchful and try to preach the sermon down into the ranks far enough so that if he is not working on Saturday night there will be someone there who understands the dangers. They're always there, and I don't think we ought to trip over ourselves out of failure to be methodical about our anticipation of our ability to screw up—not because anybody means badly, but just because we're human.

MICHAEL O'NEILL: I think there's a tremendous related issue and that's the issue of access. Perhaps more than ombudsmen, as self-appointed guardians we ought to be thinking of how to allow opposition views into the paper in response to particular issues.

Right now, for example, the networks are refusing to let businesses run what they call "advertorials," where they argue their own point of view. Newspapers are running these all the time. They're letting businessmen run opinions on public issues in their papers, for a price of course. But the networks are not allowing that to be done.

I think the op-ed pages have been a big help. But I think that perhaps we need to open up more space in the paper for groups that disagree with us or want to take another side of an issue that they don't think is getting fair representation in the press.

C.K. McCLATCHY: I'd like to put in a word of agreement with Mike on opening the paper to other views. We formalized it in Sacramento about five years ago by having something called "An Opposing View."

We found the same thing that you found—the local chairman of this group would write in. I don't think it really matters very much whether he is persuasive. I think sometimes he will be, sometimes he will not be.

But I think the important thing is that you open up the access. We've found that we have not had any real problems. Sometimes we go to the extent of soliciting an opposing view. We hear that there's somebody out there who's really bitching about an editorial. And if he's somebody who we think could write a decent piece, we will call him up and say, we understand that you have a different thought than our editorial.

If you let them have their say, even though they don't say it very well, it helps the whole process. And if you do it for enough years, I think it does have an effect. I think it helps the credibility of the paper considerably and maybe it does a real service in presenting the other side. Newspapers and television are seen as having great sway but are fantastically distrusted.